POLITICAL
GIVING

POLITICAL

GIVING

Making Sense of Individual Campaign Contributions

Bertram N. Johnson

FIRSTFORUMPRESS

A DIVISION OF LYNNE RIENNER PUBLISHERS, INC. • BOULDER & LONDON

Published in the United States of America in 2013 by
FirstForumPress
A division of Lynne Rienner Publishers, Inc.
1800 30th Street, Boulder, Colorado 80301
www.firstforumpress.com

and in the United Kingdom by
FirstForumPress
A division of Lynne Rienner Publishers, Inc.
3 Henrietta Street, Covent Garden, London WC2E 8LU

Library of Congress Cataloging-in-Publication Data
A Cataloging-in-Publication record for this book
is available from the Library of Congress.
ISBN: 978-1-935049-55-5

British Cataloguing in Publication Data
A Cataloguing in Publication record for this book
is available from the British Library.

This book was produced from digital files prepared by the author
using the FirstForumComposer.

Printed and bound in the United States of America

 The paper used in this publication meets the requirements
of the American National Standard for Permanence of
Paper for Printed Library Materials Z39.48-1992.

5 4 3 2 1

To my parents:
Campaign contributors on opposite sides of the political spectrum

Contents

Tables and Figures

Tables

Figures

Acknowledgments

This book would not have been possible without the help of many generous and able people. Thanks to the fundraising professionals who agreed to be interviewed for this project, as well as to the staff at the Federal Election Commission, who are among the most friendly and helpful people in Washington. I received valuable feedback on portions of the manuscript from my colleagues at Middlebury College, particularly Matt Dickinson, Amy Yuen, and Jeff Stauch. Thanks to Zach Drennen and Sydney Fuqua for their excellent research assistance. Thanks to those who have attended Middlebury's political science tea over the years, listened to my ideas, and challenged them productively. Thanks to my family and friends for their support. And finally, thanks to Jessica Gribble of FirstForumPress for her patience and her enthusiasm for this project. All errors are mine alone.

1

The Puzzle of Individual Giving

"A political movement and a change in the direction of government doesn't happen overnight."[1] Thus did Ron Paul in 1988 explain his quixotic Libertarian campaign for president. Speaking at Faneuil Hall in Boston, Paul, an obstetrician and sometime member of Congress, told a crowd of hundreds that "We live in an age in which the ruthlessness of the tax collector is much worse than when Sam Adams came here to complain about the taxes of Mother England."[2] The assembled crowd loved it, but the rest of the electorate proved to be skeptical: Paul garnered little more than 430,000 votes nationwide – less than half of one percent of the total votes cast that year.[3]

Two decades later, Paul ran for president again, this time in the Republican primary race. Paul's views had changed little in the intervening years. He still advocated a return to the gold standard, a dramatic reduction in the size of government, drug legalization, and a withdrawal from foreign entanglements. This time, however, his support spread in a way that was spontaneous and only partly within the candidate's control. In early fall 2007, Paul fans in internet chat rooms began buzzing about coordinating their contributions on November 5 to mark Guy Fawkes Day, the British holiday commemorating the famous Gunpowder Plot of 1605. A music promoter named Trevor Lyman – sympathetic to, but unaffiliated with, the campaign – became this idea's chief advocate. Lyman bought the domain name "ThisNovember5th.com" and launched a website.[4] Other Paul supporters spread word of the event through internet forums and conventional media outlets. When the big day came, the campaign's website provided a real-time ticker indicating how much money had been raised. The result was over $4 million in contributions from over 37,000 different people over the course of a single day.[5] A journalist at Politico.com gave the new phenomenon the clunky name "viral e-

1

bundling."[6] Paul's grassroots donors had a more colorful term: "money bomb."

The next month, Lyman organized another money bomb, this time to mark the anniversary of the Boston Tea Party. As a result, the campaign set a one-day fundraising record, tallying up over $6 million.[7] Paul, at first written off by the media as a fringe candidate who was not to be taken seriously, looked like a force to be reckoned with almost literally overnight. By the end of the primary campaign, his supporters had contributed over $34 million – more than twice as much as was raised by the more "mainstream" candidate Mike Huckabee.[8] Although he lost to John McCain in the Republican primary race, Paul far exceeded the number of votes he received in the lonely days of 1988. After he returned to Congress he garnered more attention than ever, and was sometimes credited with inspiring the Tea Party Movement that emerged in 2009.

To mark the December 2007 money bomb, crowds of supporters tramped through the Boston snow to Faneuil hall, where Ron Paul had spoken during the 1988 campaign, this time to hear a speech by his son, Rand Paul, who later won a Kentucky senate seat. The cold weather did little to mute the crowd's excitement. As one enthusiastic participant put it, "People are so engaged in this campaign because it's coming from the grass roots."[9] Paul's campaign finance record proved it.

***

In spring 2008, the Barack Obama campaign faced a choice. The Illinois senator had campaigned against his Democratic Party rival as an insurgent and a reformer. Hillary Clinton represented the old way of doing things in Washington, Obama had said in speeches and at debates, whereas Obama would set aside the stale battles of the 1990s and would move the country forward. Obama's new ideas took many forms, from his promises to prioritize environmental protection and health care, to his commitment to invest in infrastructure and technology, to his determination to "close the revolving door between government and lobbying firms" (Obama for America 2008, p. 148).

One policy statement, made in response to a November 2007 questionnaire by the reformist Midwest Democracy Network (MDN), received little attention at the time, perhaps because it seemed so in keeping with the standard repertoire of a candidate running at the head of a reform coalition within the Democratic Party. "If you are nominated for President in 2008," the MDN asked, "and your major opponents agree to forgo private funding in the general election campaign, will you participate in the presidential public financing system?"[10]

The presidential public funding system, which dates back to reforms enacted in the 1970s, seeks to keep most private money out of modern presidential campaigns by offering qualifying candidates government matching funds in primary races and (separately) a lump-sum payment to fund the general election. The subsidies are optional, however – candidates who accept the money must also agree to abide by strict spending limits. In the early years of the system's existence, candidates saw little downside to accepting this bargain. But after several decades, a growing number of presidential hopefuls concluded that the costs of modern campaigning had outstripped the resources available from public funding.[11] By the 2008 cycle, most serious candidates declined to accept matching funds in the primaries because of the onerous state-by-state spending limits with which they would have to comply. But no nominee of a major party had ever refused the lump sum payment for the fall campaign.

It was therefore probably a simple decision for the Obama campaign to answer the MDN in the affirmative back in 2007, promising to accept the lump sum payment if Obama won the nomination. After all, it fit with the campaign's reformist self-image. "Yes," replied Obama to the public financing question. "I have been a long-time advocate for public financing of campaigns combined with free television and radio time as a way to reduce the influence of moneyed special interests." Furthermore, "If I am the Democratic nominee, I will aggressively pursue an agreement with the Republican nominee to preserve a publicly financed general election."[12]

That was in November 2007. But then something unexpected happened: the Obama campaign turned out to be good at raising money on its own. Exceptionally good. Month after month, the Obama fundraising effort bested Hillary Clinton in dollar amounts – Hillary Clinton, who had at her disposal a network of elite fundraisers that she and her husband had cultivated for nearly two decades. Wealthy fundraisers played a significant role in the Obama effort as well, which was no surprise. No major presidential campaign effort can survive without them. What was startling, however, was the extent to which small individual contributions poured into the campaign. Each new milestone – positive and negative alike – seemed to stoke the fires further. After Obama won the Iowa Caucuses, $6 million flowed into the campaign website by the next morning, (Plouffe 2010, p. 140). After Obama lost the New Hampshire primary to Clinton, undaunted online contributors handed him his best 24 hours of fundraising yet (Plouffe

2010, p. 154). By June 2008 (as FEC data show), the Obama campaign had raised far more than any previous presidential campaign: $366 million. To put that amount in perspective, the highest spending previous primary campaign was that of George W. Bush in 2004. Bush had fallen short of Obama's total by nearly $100 million.[13]

Now, with the primary season behind them, Obama and his staff had to decide whether to abide by the previous year's idealistic pledge. The lump sum public funding payment for the fall campaign would be $85 million. Obama's fundraisers were confident that if the campaign opted out, they could raise two or three times that much. Furthermore, if the campaign accepted public funding, many private donors would give instead to the Democratic Party, a separate organization that might not spend these funds in a way that harmonized well with the campaign (Plouffe 2010).

A cynic would say that self interest beat out principle: On June 19, the campaign announced that it would forego the matching funds and raise money privately for the general election. The Republican presumptive nominee, John McCain (a reformer himself), announced that he would take the funds, and proceeded to lambast Obama for breaking his word.

Obama argued, however, that he had not abandoned his reformist orientation. Focusing on the smallest contributions, the candidate argued that his campaign itself represented a reform of sorts. Addressing his supporters, he said, "Instead of forcing us to rely on millions from Washington lobbyists and special interest PACs, you've fueled this campaign with donations of $5, $10, $20, whatever you can afford. And because you did, we've built a grassroots movement of over 1.5 million Americans. ...You've already changed the way campaigns are funded because you know that's the only way we can truly change how Washington works."[14] In another statement, Obama even likened his small contributor base to a "parallel public financing system."[15] Chief strategist David Axelrod explained: "The campaign finance system was constructed in order to reduce the influence of large donations...Here it's happening naturally: people are sending $5, $10, $25, $100 contributions."[16] The reform goal had not changed, the campaign argued – it was the nature of the reform that had evolved in an unexpected way.

***

Why did so many people contribute to the Ron Paul and Barack Obama presidential campaigns? More broadly, what motivates those who give money to campaigns and causes? Has the number of small contributors increased over time, as Obama implied in his explanation for rejecting public funds? How does the campaign finance environment affect – and reflect – the political environment in the United States? In this book, I explore these questions using historical documents, interviews with fundraising professionals, campaign finance data, and public opinion surveys.

Previous works of scholarship and public policy have not answered these important questions. If the Ron Paul and Barack Obama examples are any indication, something new may be happening in the campaign finance world that has not been addressed by those who studied the system in the 1980s or 1990s. Most mass-market books on the campaign finance system focus on the relationship between special interests and elected officials (usually members of Congress), arguing that a corrupt collusion has given Americans "The Best Congress Money Can Buy" or a "Hostile Takeover" by special interests (Stern 1988, Sirota 2006). Scholarship in political science and economics, while reaching less alarming conclusions, has focused on similar questions regarding the relationships between contributors and elected officials. What effects do contributions from special interests have on the policy-making process? What do interested parties receive in exchange for their contributions? How likely is a politician to shift his or her policy stance in response to a hefty contribution?

Although the issues raised by these questions are important, I focus here on equally important, but more often neglected questions. My focus stems from two key points. First, contributions from special interests are by no means the only source of campaign funds in the United States. Individual contributions – not contributions from corporate Political Action Committees (PACs) – are the main source of funds for congressional candidates, parties, and presidential candidates alike. Some of these individuals may represent special interests. But many may not. We would probably not call the millions of Ron Paul and Barack Obama contributors "special interests," yet these contributors – and others like them – were vitally important in shaping the 2008 and 2012 presidential races.

Second, raising money for political campaigns and causes is hard work. Contributors do not simply come knocking on the candidate's door (in most cases). As any finance director on a congressional campaign understands, it takes a tremendous amount of effort to generate the funds necessary to run for office – whether it be for a state legislative seat or the presidency. Contrary to some popular misconceptions, money does not simply show up at the doorstep. Decades ago, when campaigns were nowhere near as expensive as they are today, Hubert Humphrey famously called fundraising a "disgusting, degrading, demeaning experience" (Adamany & Agree 1975, p. 8). If politicians simply had to hold court and wait for the money to roll in, it would not be so bad.

In the remainder of this chapter, I lay the foundation for the rest of the book by developing these two points. Individual contributions are important in U.S. political campaigns, and they are growing more numerous. This phenomenon is an especially puzzling one because many individuals appear to have no obvious incentives to donate. This lack of clear reasons to give explains why campaigns often have to work so hard to raise money. Next, I introduce a theoretical framework first suggested by the political scientists Peter Clark and James Q. Wilson to offer a useful preliminary understanding of why people may contribute to political campaigns and causes. Finally, I provide a brief outline of the rest of the book.

How Many Contributors?

In 2008 candidates for federal office (president, Senate, and House of Representatives) raised about $3.2 billion, according to data available at the Federal Election Commission, and more than two-thirds of this amount came from individuals. In the 2010 congressional races, held during a time of high unemployment and economic stagnation, candidates raised fully $2.1 billion – $1.2 billion (or about 60 percent) from individuals. When the final numbers for the 2012 cycle are tallied, the amounts raised will undoubtedly top $4 billion, again mostly donated by individual contributors – even in a time of economic hardship and slow GDP growth. Despite all the attention given to contributions from corporate, labor, and interest group PACs, it is difficult to escape the conclusion that, as one group of political scientists put it, "individuals, rather than organizations, are by far the most important source of campaign funds" (Ansolabehere, de Figuerido & Snyder 2003, p. 109).

Not only do individuals make up the majority of contributors to political campaigns, but their number has been increasing in recent years. To be sure, nowhere near a majority of Americans gives money to candidates for office. But while as little as seven percent told pollsters they donated money to politics in the early 1990s, by 2008 this figure had nearly doubled, to almost 13 percent, as Figure 1.1 shows. By comparison, only nine percent said they had attended a political meeting, and only four percent claimed to have worked to support a candidate or cause. Aside from voting, therefore, contributing money is

Figure 1.1: Individual Contributions Have Increased Since the 1990s

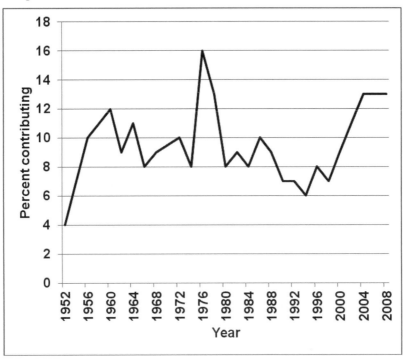

Source: American National Election Studies.

one of the primary ways in which Americans participate in politics.[17] If we extrapolate from these survey-based figures, nearly 28 million Americans were campaign contributors in 2008.[18] Even if there is an over-reporting rate of around 20 percent, as there tends to be for voter turnout, for example, this works out to more than 22 million contributors. This is a number larger than the entire population of Florida. For decades, political scientists have examined the question of why people vote; the question of why people contribute is important enough to deserve similar scrutiny.

The Nature of the Puzzle

Many readers might be skeptical that there is any mystery to the question of why people give money to politics. People give to candidates and groups because they believe in the causes with which candidates and groups associate themselves. Contributors simply want to improve the chances that their preferred candidates or causes will succeed. Indeed, if you approached a typical "person on the street" and asked her why people contribute, this is very likely to be the answer that you would receive.

As with many first attempts at a scholarly understanding of a common phenomenon, the first political scientists to study the question of why individuals engage in political activity came to conclusions quite similar to this conventional wisdom. David Truman, a political scientist at Columbia University (and later the president of Mount Holyoke College), developed such a point of view in his classic 1951 book, *The Governmental Process*. Although Truman's work concerns the question of why people join and contribute to political groups, his analysis is instructive for the question of campaign contributions, since this, too, can represent a form of group affiliation. My contribution to a campaign makes me a member of the overall campaign effort. Modern campaigns recognize this by congratulating contributors for joining the "team."

Drawing in part on previous work by Arthur Bentley, Truman reasoned that groups (or, as we might put it today, "interest groups") were centrally important to politics because they were the main way in which people made an impact on the policy-making process. Groups were characterized by people who had common interests – in lower taxes, greater spending on social services, the opening up of more public lands to rock climbing, or whatever. Many groups – perhaps even most groups – were "latent" – they were inactive because their interests were not directly at stake in current political debates. When issues arose in politics that concerned group interests, however, groups became "manifest" – they leaped into action to defend their goals. The overall governmental process, therefore, was one in which groups with competing interests fought their battles in the arena of public policy-making institutions. The result was that policy outcomes were basically fair – they took into account the interests of all relevant groups.

This simple and compelling argument about group organization has obvious implications for our understanding of campaign finance. Truman's answer to the question of why people contribute to candidates would be that a political contribution represents an individual's decision to change a latent group affiliation into a manifest one. When people see their interests as being threatened, or when they see an opportunity to advance their interests, they take action to support the group's political goals. This action could include joining a membership association, but very often in our modern society, political action takes the form of monetary contributions. A group that advocates a particular policy is an obvious potential beneficiary of such contributions, but candidates and parties that promise to promote the same policy might be equally likely to win the support of interested contributors.

This account makes intuitive sense – our person on the street would no doubt agree with it wholeheartedly. It also seems to explain some of the phenomena we see in the world of contributions. The most obvious examples concern cases in which apparent threats to group interests suddenly appear. In 2011, for example, when Indiana Governor Mitch Daniels signed a bill ending state funding of Planned Parenthood because of the organization's abortion services, donations to Planned Parenthood surged.[19] After Florida Governor Charlie Crist embraced the Obama Administration's economic stimulus package funds, his more conservative opponent in the Republican Senate primary, Marco Rubio, amassed a quick $3.6 million in individual gifts.[20] And after the Supreme Court ruled the Obama health care bill constitutional in 2012, contributions to Republican presidential candidate Mitt Romney and to the Democratic Congressional Campaign Committee skyrocketed.[21]

These kinds of giving patterns might indeed be interpreted in terms of contributors who wish to improve the chances that their views will prevail in the public sphere. But if one thinks a bit more carefully about what it would take to affect the outcome of a policy making process, as a generation of political scientists beginning with Mancur Olson did, this view of the world seems incomplete. Olson pointed out that public policy preferences concern collective goods – goods that apply to all members of a relevant group, and that cannot be denied to anyone if the good is provided at all. In most such cases, Olson reasoned, individuals would see that their own contributions would have little effect on the outcome, and would rationally decline to contribute to a collective good's provision.

Consider the following thought experiment. Would you prefer that the sides of roads and the parks near where you live be free of litter? Of course you would – like most people, you probably place value on the aesthetics of your surroundings, and you also may object in principle to the pollution of the natural environment. Now, think of the last time you have cleaned up some litter on the side of the road or in a public park. When was that? Perhaps, like many people, you have no time to spend on such tasks due to work, family, school, or other obligations. In that case, when was the last time you paid $25 into a fund designated for cleanup?

Olson would not fault you if you sheepishly answered "never" to both of those questions. In fact, he would see it as a rational response to a situation involving a collective good (outdoor green space). Note that

Truman would have expected you to leap into action: if your interests are at stake, you get involved. Olson, on the other hand, would expect you to give only under very rare circumstances. If your contribution makes the difference between provision and non-provision of the good – between whether litter is cleaned up or whether it is left to accumulate – then Olson expects a rational individual to chip in. Absent such unique circumstances, you'll keep your money.

Herein lies the crux of the puzzle: the election of one's preferred candidate or the enactment of one's preferred policy is a collective good, just like green space in the example above. So, considering the fact that an individual contribution to a political campaign is unlikely to be the deciding factor in an election, why should anyone donate money to a candidate or cause? To be sure, we could imagine a circumstance in which an individual contribution would be decisive – insurance magnate W. Clement Stone contributed over $2 million to Richard Nixon's 1972 reelection effort, for example – the equivalent of over $11 million in today's dollars (Alexander 1976, 73). This amount might very well have had the potential to affect the outcome of the race, although the 1972 campaign could have been decided by any number of factors. But modern campaign finance rules would appear to preclude instances of such decisiveness. Current law limits individual contributors to (as of 2012) a $2,500 contribution to a primary campaign and a $2,500 contribution to a general election campaign. A typical victorious House race costs $1 million; a winning Senate race $5 million; and presidential races cost hundreds of millions of dollars. In light of such costly campaigns, $5,000 seems like a paltry sum – hardly enough to make or break a candidate's chances.[22]

Furthermore, the vast majority of individual contributions never approach this maximum amount. The Federal Election Commission does not require candidates to itemize contributions below $200, so the average contribution level is impossible to know with precision. Still, candidates for Congress report raising nearly a quarter of their funds from individuals in amounts less than $200. Fully 43 percent of money raised from individuals comes from donations of less than $750.[23] The 2008 Obama presidential campaign estimated its average contribution as being under $100 (Plouffe 2010, 261). No single one of these small contributions could realistically be said to have a chance at affecting the outcome of an election. It does not make sense for people to contribute if changing the outcome of the election is their goal.

It is important to stress that this logic applies even if (potential) contributors are strong supporters of a candidate or cause. No matter how strongly you feel about something, your estimate of the probability that your contribution will be decisive will be tiny. Just as a proponent of clean parks and litter-free streets might rationally presume his or her contribution will have no impact on the overall condition of parks and streets, a candidate's supporters should rationally make a similar estimation regarding a campaign contribution. Candidates, parties, and interest groups all face a collective action problem: their supporters have little incentive to contribute to their 'victory funds.' So how is it possible to mobilize people into politics when they have no obvious incentive to get involved?

Much of the political science literature on interest groups has focused on strategies that interest group leaders have used to goad people into participation (e.g. Moe 1980). Candidates for office also often employ similar techniques. One common practice, for example, is for leaders and candidates to exaggerate the 'decisiveness' of each contribution. The micro-lending website Kiva has done extraordinarily well at linking each contribution to a "decisive" effect on an individual or small group in a developing country. Here is an account of one prospective loan recipient featured on Kiva's website:

> María is 26 years old; she is married and has a child. She works selling products, in a food stall…. She buys the products she needs in a city in the eastern side of the country that is about fifteen minutes away from her house, by car. [She is requesting a loan to] buy another food stall, and she wants to supply it with candy, beverages, fast food, etc. to generate more income since the first food stall produced good profits. … This will allow her to earn a higher income, to provide her child with an education and for the new member of the family who will be born soon..[24]

After reading this account, a potential contributor is likely to believe that his or her contribution will make a real difference in this person's life. Campaigns have a tougher job of making each contribution seem decisive, but that does not stop them from trying. As each election cycle develops, voters receive emails, letters, and flyers implying that the race hangs by a thread and that just one more contribution could help win the day. A July 2012 email from the Romney campaign to his supporters declares:

> There are 100 days left until Election Day. To defeat Barack Obama, his liberal allies and their reelection machine in November, every day and every donation will count. Donate $100 today - one dollar for each day remaining - and together we can take back the White House in

November, make Barack Obama a one-term president, and defeat his liberal allies.[25]

An Obama campaign email sent at about the same time delivers an urgent message as well:

> Don't let anyone persuade you that this is a sure thing - our opponents have almost unlimited resources at their disposal, and we already know they'll outspend us by a good amount. What we do now decides the headlines on November 7th. We're facing a huge fundraising deadline. Please donate now, and have a hand in the outcome of this election.[26]

The scholarly work focused on the efforts of campaigns and interest groups to attract supporters has generated many valuable insights, some of which I explore in later sections of this book. But to focus the question on what successful interest group leaders do elides the key question of why individuals decide to do what they do. To credit the 'exaggerated decisiveness' leadership strategy, for instance, is to suggest that contributors give to campaigns and causes because they are being systematically deceived. This may be so, but it is a claim that needs to be tested empirically. Successful and unsuccessful leadership strategies provide some important clues as to why individuals donate, but they are no substitute for a direct answer to this question.

Another possible way of spurring potential contributors' participation is to appeal to their self-interest by coercing them or bribing them. There is no shortage of examples of such tactics in U.S. history and in other electoral systems around the world. In "union shop" states, employees who wish to work in certain industries must join unions. In machine politics systems of the past, political campaigns provided so-called "walking around money" to campaign activists who in turn paid voters for their trouble. But most of these avenues are closed to political actors these days, at least in the United States. Although outright bribery and hard-nosed coercion may sometimes be present, their perpetrators usually risk prosecution, so the incidence of such behavior is likely to be too low to explain the large number of individual campaign contributions that we observe in modern campaigns.

Political scientists Peter Clark and James Q. Wilson, in a classic article (Clark and Wilson 1961), proposed a framework for understanding why individuals might see it as being in their self interest to join or support groups, despite the lack of apparent incentives to do so. Wilson expanded on this theory later in a well-known book (Wilson 1995 [1974]). I will delve more deeply into Wilson's ideas in the next chapter, but Wilson's main point was that potential contributors needed so-called "selective incentives" in order to make it worth their while. Such incentives operated with a softer touch than traditional bribery or coercion, but did make it worthwhile for donors to take action, or punished them for non-action. To be effective, these incentives should apply to contributors, but not to non contributors, ensuring that a collective good is in some sense linked to a private good. People have clear incentives to pursue private goods – they do so every time they go to the grocery store. So if campaigns and causes can offer private goods of some kind in connection with their campaigns, they may be able to rationalize the irrational.

Wilson's insight was that these incentives might not be as obvious as casual observers would think. There are three general types of selective incentives, Wilson argued. First, material incentives could include bribes, but might also include more minor tangible rewards to participation. Members of the American Automobile Association get a magazine and hotel discounts, for example. Membership in the AARP provides access to cheap insurance. Material incentives such as these can tip the balance in a potential donor's calculations, and make it much more likely for him or her to contribute.

Even more subtle are two other types of selective incentives. A second type, "solidary" incentives (a term reminiscent of the 'solidarity' one feels with other like-minded people) are the benefits conferred from associating with people with whom one wants to associate. For some, this might mean the ability to hang out with dignitaries or other notables. No doubt this rationale is behind the common practice of the "dinner fundraiser," at which contributors gather to eat and mingle with the candidate and his or her associates. Solidary incentives can also be powerful motivators for members of a group that sees itself as outnumbered or besieged in some way. When Howard Dean supporters began organizing "MeetUps" (using the newly-founded website of the same name) in 2003 near the height of the George W. Bush administration's popularity, liberal participants were exhilarated to meet others who swam against the tide. When conservative organizers staged Tea Party rallies in 2009, foes of the Obama administration felt the same way. "Sometimes you don't know how many people you know until you come down here," one activist at a national Tea Party event told a reporter. "We have friends now across the country. It's amazing" (Zernike 2010, p. 122). Social benefits, while difficult to quantify, are nonetheless real, and may provide a partial explanation of why some people contribute to candidates or causes, despite Olson's free rider problem.

   Third, Wilson outlined a type of incentive he called "purposive." By this, he meant that some people contribute to a cause because they would feel worse about themselves if they did nothing. Note that this is not the same thing as supporting a candidate or cause because one wants to affect the outcome. For a purposive incentive to work, a person must feel bad about him or herself if he or she does not make a contribution. It is the difference between "I prefer clean parks" and "I'm a bad person if I don't help the parks." Another way to think about it would be to see a purposive incentive wherever it is possible for a person to say "no matter what the outcome of this election (or of this policy debate), I will feel happier having contributed than not having contributed." National Public Radio's fundraising drives frequently target this type of incentive.[27] Martin Luther King, Jr. also did so when he argued that "We will have to repent in this generation not merely for the vitriolic words and actions of the bad people, but for the appalling silence of the good people."[28] What self-identified "good person" could hear such a call and fail to feel guilty at his or her own inaction?

   While solidary incentives are difficult to quantify, purposive incentives would seem nearly impossible to identify clearly for any large number of people. Furthermore, can it be possible that this category could lead to millions of Americans not just joining groups, voting, or taking part in other minimally-demanding forms of participation, but spending money on something that promises no tangible return?

   Olson's puzzle and Wilson's framework of incentives shows us that the job of the campaign fundraiser is more difficult and complex than it would appear at first glance. Contrary to what David Truman argued, and to what most people would assume at first blush, it is a surprise that anyone contributes money to political campaigns. That enough people do so to sustain the current campaign finance system is nothing short of astonishing.

   As Wilson suggested, part of the reason that campaigns are able to collect funds is that they do their best to make such contributions attractive to potential donors. In other words, they offer selective incentives. Just as interest group strategies differ from group to group, different campaigns are likely to offer different combinations of selective incentives. Similarly, different prospective contributors may respond to different selective incentives. The combination of the "demand side" strategies of political campaigns and the "supply side" characteristics of prospective contributors produces the complex campaign finance system that we have today, and guides the inquiry in the rest of this book.

Preview of the Book

The remainder of this book examines the puzzle of individual political giving in more detail. It is a particularly important puzzle to be dealing with at the current moment in American politics for several reasons. First, the number of individual contributors has been rising, as I pointed out at the beginning of this introduction. This suggests that for some reason, campaign contributions have become a more attractive option for an increasing number of Americans. We would be wise to pay attention to this growing form of political engagement.

Second, this increase may also have something to tell us about the way in which politics can interact with – and be changed by – the surrounding context. It is difficult to observe the rising trend in contributing in the early 21st century and not connect it to the rise of the internet. Indeed, the Ron Paul and Barack Obama campaigns would have found it much more difficult to achieve what they did in the absence of online contributing. Further innovations such as the Federal Election Commission's 2012 decision to allow political contributions via text message seem likely to make contributions easier still. Has new technology fundamentally changed Americans' relationship with politics? Or does the new technology simply represent the natural extension of previously-existing trends?

Third, it is important to examine the role of individual contributions in the particularly polarized political environment in modern U.S. politics. Political scientists have thoroughly documented the current polarization among politicians and political activists, and many have also puzzled over whether this polarization is reflected in the mass electorate (Fiorina 2011; Levendusky 2009; McCarty, Poole & Rosenthal 2006). If voters remain moderate while politicians polarize, as some have claimed, there are serious implications for the quality of representation in the U.S. Like those who study polarization, scholars who study campaign finance are often fundamentally concerned with issues of representation. At the extreme, if a politician ignores his or her constituents in favor of doing the bidding of a wealthy donor, representation would appear to have failed. Political scientists have studied the representation question as concerns special interest groups such as Political Action Committees. But what are the implications of the large and growing number of individual contributions for representation?

Some analysts – echoing the 2008 Obama campaign – argue that increasing the number of small individual contributions will improve representation by making the typical contributor more similar to the typical voter. As *American Prospect* author Mark Schmitt put it, "Such a broad and diverse base of donors and the astonishing percentage of small donors [in the 2008 campaigns]… have to significantly alleviate concerns about corruption resulting from the leverage that any individual donor, group of donors, or major fundraiser would hold." Accordingly, writes Schmitt, campaign finance reforms should "create every incentive for small donors to participate and for candidates and parties to seek small donors."[29]

Others argue, however, that a system that favors small contributions would exacerbate problems of representation. Former FEC Chairman Bradley Smith observes that "In many cases, those candidates who are best able to raise campaign dollars in small contributions are those who are most emphatically out of the mainstream of their time." After all, Ron Paul seemed far from the mainstream during his first campaign in 1988, but won the support of thousands of small contributors two decades later, when technology made it easier to reach out to small contributors. Smith argues that fringe candidates can succeed with small contributors because "collective action problems may be overcome in some instances by a radical campaign in which donors are motivated by strong ideologies" (Smith 2001, 46-47). Purposive incentives, in other words, encourage candidates to appeal to a radical minority. If Smith is right, a rising tide of small contributions could make the system less representative rather than more so.

The remainder of this book will shed light on these important issues in the context of the modern campaign finance environment. In Chapter 2 I delve more deeply into academic theories about why people might contribute to candidates or causes. The simple framework that James Q. Wilson proposed has been developed, modified and altered in different ways by political scientists, economists, psychologists, and sociologists. Each tradition has valuable insights to add to the puzzle, and a review of this literature leads to a concrete series of expectations about what we should find in data on individual contributions. Crucially, not all of these expectations are compatible with one another, but their specificity allows scholars to test them with existing data.

In Chapters 3 and 4, I review the modern campaign finance landscape, beginning with a brief history of fundraising in the United States, and discussing 30 years' worth of data on campaign finance with an eye towards the role played by individual contributions. A discussion of how campaign fundraising has changed and developed over time will better help us to understand how fundraisers view their task as well as why individuals contribute to politics. Much of the modern campaign finance system can be traced to the lessons learned by fundraisers from historical campaigns, as well as from the parallel worlds of marketing and philanthropic giving. In these chapters I rely on historical documents, more recent aggregate data from the Federal Election Commission, and interviews with experienced fundraisers. The context provided by this discussion sets the stage for a more detailed quantitative analysis of how fundraising works today.

In Chapters 5 and 6, I examine this data. Chapter 5 focuses on campaign finance data for congressional campaigns available from the Federal Election Commission (FEC). These data allow us to determine which types of candidates are more successful in raising money from individuals. Chapter 6 focuses on survey data from the American National Election Studies to test our expectations about which Americans are more likely to contribute and which are less likely to do so.

Finally, in Chapters 7 and 8, I draw conclusions about individual contributions and about the campaign finance system as a whole. In Chapter 7, I sum up findings from the previous chapters and piece them together to paint a coherent picture of individual giving in the context of a changing campaign finance environment. In Chapter 8, I discuss the implications of this picture for the future of the campaign finance system. Should reformers seek to elevate the importance of individual contributions? Should they seek a balance between small individual contributions, large individual contributions, and contributions from interest groups? Or should they seek to eliminate private money from the campaign finance system altogether? The answers to these questions are not as clear as they seem.

---

[1] Bob Davis, "Libertarian Party's Ron Paul Offers Platform Based on Polite Anarchism," *Wall Street Journal*, November 4, 1988, p. A16.

[2] Ibid.

[3] Dave Leip's Atlas of U.S. Presidential Elections, http://uselectionatlas.org/.

[4] Kenneth P. Vogel, "The man, the technique, behind Paul's haul," *Politico.com*, November 6, 2007.

[5] Dan Morain, "The unlikely man behind Paul's fundraising curtain," *Los Angeles Times*, December 16, 2007, http://articles.latimes.com /2007/dec/16/nation/na-moneyman16, accessed June 6, 2011; Jose Antonio Vargas, "Paul's Money-Bomb Throwers," http://voices.washingtonpost.com /44/2007/11/post-184.html, accessed June 6, 2011.

[6] Vogel, "The Man…".

[7] Kenneth Vogel, "Ron Paul becomes $6 million man," *Politico.com*, December 17, 2007.

[8]   OpenSecrets.org, http://www.opensecrets.org/pres08/alsorans. php, accessed June 6, 2011.

[9] Michael Levenson, "Ron Paul backers stage Boston Tea Party, raise millions," *Boston Globe*, December 17, 2007, p. A12.

[10] Midwest Democracy Network, "Edwards and Obama Detail Reform Plans; Midwest Civic Group Releases Results of Presidential Questionnaire," press release, November 27, 2007, http://www.commoncause.org/atf/cf/%7Bfb3c17e2-cdd1-4df6-92be-bd44298936 65%7D/MDNNATIONALRELEASE.PDF, accessed June 10, 2011.

[11] Public funds are indexed to inflation, but campaign spending tends to increase at rates that exceed the inflation rate.

[12] Midwest Democracy Network.

[13] "2008 Presidential Campaign Finance Activity Summarized," Federal Election Commission, June 8, 2009, http://fec.gov/press/press2009/20090608PresStat.shtml, accessed June 20, 2011.

[14] Jake Tapper, "Obama to Break Promise, Opt Out of Public Financing for General Election," ABC News, http://blogs.abcnews.com/politicalpunch/2008/06/obama-to-break.html, accessed June 10, 2011.

[15] Jeff Zeleny & Michael Luo, "Public Financing? Obama and McCain Appear Split," *New York Times*, April 10, 2008, p. A19.

[16] Zeleny & Luo.

[17] More people – about 20 percent – wear a button or put a bumper sticker on their car. But this activity is relatively costless compared with contributing money.

[18] Based on 13 percent of a voting eligible population of 213.2 million. VEP figure available at The United States Elections Project, George Mason University, http://elections.gmu.edu/index.html.

[19] Laura Bassett, "Indiana Planned Parenthood Sees Flood of Donations After Defunding," Huffington Post, May 16, 2011, http://www.huffingtonpost.com/2011/05/16/indiana-planned-parenthood-defunded_n_862423.html.

[20] Aaron Deslatte, "Marco Rubio Campaign raises three times more than Charlie Crist in quarter," Orlando Sentinel, April 9, 2010, http://articles.orlandosentinel.com/2010-04-09/news/os-crist-contribution-total-20100409_1_federal-stimulus-bailout-crist-campaign-marco-rubio.

[21] Rachel Streitfield & Kevin Bohn, "Fund Raising Flurry after Supreme Court Ruling," CNN Political Ticker, June 29, 2012, http://politicalticker.blogs.cnn.com/2012/06/29/fund-raising-flurry-after-supreme-court-ruling/; Joshua Miller, "DCCC Fundraising Surges Since Supreme Court Decision on Health Care," *Roll Call*, July 3, 2012, http://atr.rollcall.com/dccc-fundraising-surges-since-supreme-court-decision-on-health-care/.

[22] The 2012 race, in which a few wealthy individuals donated millions to so-called "Super PACs" might also seem to provide cases in which an individual could be decisive. Even in 2012, however, most political money came in far smaller amounts. Furthermore, even large contributions are no guarantee of decisiveness. Casino magnate Sheldon Adelson's preferred candidate in the Republican primary race, Newt Gingrich, lost despite Adelson's contributions of over $20 million to a pro-Gingrich Super PAC.

[23] These calculations are the author's, based on the FEC's 2006 Candidate Financial Summaries (End of Cycle), available at http://fec.gov/finance /disclosure/ftpsum.shtml.

[24] Kiva website, http://www.kiva.org/lend/445181, accessed August 13, 2012.

[25] ProPublica, http://projects.propublica.org/emails/mailings/100-days, accessed August 13, 2012.

[26] ProPublica, http://projects.propublica.org/emails/mailings/obama-defeats-romney, accessed August 13, 2012.

[27] For an analysis of how social norms may condition 'tastes' for contributing to NPR, see Martha Kropf and Stephen Knack, "Viewers Like You: Community Norms and Contributions to Public Broadcasting," *Political Research Quarterly* 56:2 (June 2003), pp. 187-197.

[28] In "Letter from Birmingham City Jail," Martin Luther King, Jr. A Testament of Hope: The Essential Writings and Speeches of Martin Luther King, Jr. (New York: Harper Collins, 1986), p. 296. King used variants of this phrase repeatedly in his writings and speeches.

[29] Mark Schmitt, "Can Money Be a Force for Good? The Revolutionary Potential of Small-Donor Democracy," *The American Prospect* 20:1 (January-February 2009), p. A13.

2

Competing Theories of Individual Participation

I began this book with a simple question: Why do people contribute money to political campaigns and causes? As I discussed in the introduction, the first scholarly response to this question was that people naturally contribute when their interests are at stake in one public policy debate or another. But after the publication of Mancur Olson's *Logic of Collective Action*, this began to look like an unsatisfactory answer (Olson 1965). The collective action problem renders it irrational in most cases for an individual to contribute to a collective good.

Scholars since Olson have addressed this collective action problem in various ways. In this chapter, I review the principal ways in which previous research seeks to solve the puzzle of why individuals contribute at all – and especially why so many individuals give what to candidates (and even to contributors) must appear to be trivial amounts. I first sketch out three broader categories of explanation, and then go into greater detail on each one.

One obvious initial reaction to the puzzle of individual contributions is that people contribute to campaigns and causes because they get tangible benefits in return. This explanation addresses the challenge posed by the collective action logic by positing that some private good changes hands in conjunction with – and conditional upon – the individual contributions to the collective good. If, as Olson argues, most people have no rational incentive to contribute to collective goods, then those who do in fact contribute must be doing so because of their own self interest.

To the extent that these benefits quantifiable in economic terms, James Q. Wilson classified them as "material incentives." Material incentives may indeed be an important component in why some people contribute to candidates. This is most likely to be true of contributors who have clear material interests at stake, and who can contribute amounts that make it plausible that a candidate or party will take notice of their contribution. If money buys "access," as many scholars suspect, this access may in turn lead to something valuable: votes on legislation (Stratmann 1991), the rescinding of threatened regulation (McChesney 1997), or committee work on behalf of a contributor (Hall and Wayman 1990). Among the constellation of those who give to political campaigns, Political Action Committees and large individual contributors are most likely to have material motives. They have the resources as well as the motivation to vie for something tangible in exchange for their help. Those who contribute smaller amounts are less likely to be motivated by such interests, however. It is unlikely that those who contribute $25 or even $100 do so in the expectation of changing a candidate's behavior in office.

Contributions may also be motivated by social, or "solidary" rewards (in James Q. Wilson's terms). They may serve as a "membership fee" to an exclusive club that certain contributors are anxious to join. When members of this club gather at fundraisers or "meetups," for example, contributors may reap the benefits of the 'weak ties' that these associations create (Granovetter 1973), or they may simply derive enjoyment from associating with people who are similar to them. PACs may be motivated by solidary incentives if CEOs of the affiliated companies enjoy hobnobbing with elected officials (Clawson, Neustadtl & Weller 1998). In certain cases, large individual contributions guarantee entry to fundraising dinners or other social events.

Smaller individual contributions may or may not be associated with social rewards. In rare cases, even a minimal contribution can garner access to a candidate. In 2011, for example, the Obama campaign entered its June contributors of $25 or more into a lottery to win lunch with President Obama and Vice President Biden. More commonly, small contributions may be made as one in a number of activities associated with membership in a local political group or association. The social ties associated with these organizations can be brought to bear as social pressure when it comes time to contribute. In recent years, colleges and universities have had great success in alumni fundraising when classmates solicit other classmates, for example. As political scientist Robert Putnam puts it, "Fund-raising typically means friend-raising" (Putnam 2000, p. 121). Members of localized groups with political agendas (such as the National Rifle Association or the Sierra Club) may work the same way.

Figure 2.1: Number of Reported Contributions from Individuals vs. PACs and Parties, 1980-2008

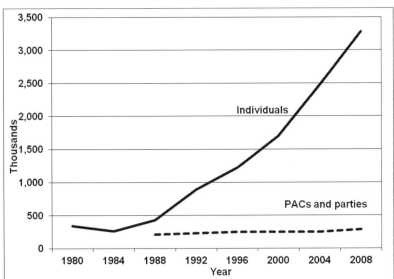

Source: Federal Election Commission, www.fec.gov.

Finally, people may contribute to the provision of a collective good to receive what James Q. Wilson called "purposive" incentives: "intangible rewards that derive from the sense of satisfaction of having contributed to the attainment of a worthwhile cause" (Wilson 1974, p. 34). In contrast to material and solidary incentives, the "purposive" incentive does not have a well-developed explanation in the logic of self interest. Empirical studies of purposive incentives have found that they appear to be important, but that they come in many varieties (Hildreth 1994, Whiteley & Seyd 2002, Cebula, Durden & Gaynor 2008).

The issue of intangible incentives takes on growing importance in the current political environment, in which an increasing number of Americans contribute to political campaigns in the absence of any clear material or social motive. As Figure 1.1 in Chapter 1 shows, the percentage of people surveyed who report having made political contributions has nearly doubled since 2000. Figure 2.1 shows the number of individual contributions reported to the Federal Election

Commission since 1980. Although reporting is incomplete because candidates are not required to itemize the smallest contributions (those below $200), the dramatic rise in this figure (especially when compared with the essentially constant number of contributions from PACs and parties), corresponds with what the survey data show.

Candidates for federal office in 2008 raised a total of approximately $3.2 billion, according to the Federal Election Commission (FEC). Roughly 68 percent of this money came from individual contributions, while only 13 percent came from Political Action Committees. Some of these individuals no doubt contribute because of social or material reasons. A corporate CEO or lobbyist may expect to meet with the candidate in exchange for a $2,000 contribution, or an activist may see a $100 contribution as her ticket to social events and other political gatherings. But the large number of small contributions should direct our focus not just at material and solidary incentives, but at intangible incentives as well. Officials from Barack Obama's presidential campaign, for example, claimed that their average contribution was $90. It strains credibility to argue that those who contributed $25 over the internet did so to receive material –or even social – rewards. Political scientists have demonstrated that at least some individuals contribute for reasons that do not appear to be social or material (McCarty, Pool, & Rosenthal 2006; Francia et al. 2003), and that the tendency to contribute for intangible reasons appears to be greater among those who give the smallest contributions (Johnson 2010).

Political scientists therefore ought to think just as carefully about intangible incentives as they have about social and material incentives if their understanding of the campaign finance environment is to be complete. Only by developing very clear empirical predictions about each of these types of incentives – and then testing them against available evidence – will we be able to understand one of the most important features of the modern campaign finance environment.

In the remainder of this chapter, I review the different, often parallel, lines of thinking about incentives for participation in collective activity, some from political science, others from sociology, psychology, and economics.

There are systematic differences in the way that scholars have thought about the incentives that drive individual contributions to collective goods. These differences allow us to generate specific hypotheses about fundraising patterns that can be tested with the available data. After discussing material and solidary incentives, I identify three analytically distinct categories of intangible incentives: "purposive" incentives, socially-defined expressive incentives, and emotionally-defined expressive incentives. I derive specific hypotheses on how each of these categories of incentives might be linked to contributions, and speculate on how each theoretical approach would explain the recent growth in campaign giving among individuals. This sets the stage for the analysis of the historical record (Chapter 3), of modern campaigns (Chapter 4), of campaign finance reports (Chapter 5) and of survey data (Chapter 6) that I will undertake in the rest of the book.

When such an analysis operationalizes each type of incentive separately, it becomes easier to pinpoint how and why the campaign finance environment may be changing. Nevertheless, despite the analytical distinctiveness of each kind of incentive, it is possible – and indeed likely – that contributing to candidates and causes are in many cases due to combinations of two or more different types of incentives.

To provide a complete account of the incentives facing potential contributors, I begin by considering material incentives, move on to discuss solidary incentives, and spend the bulk of the chapter focusing on the less well understood category of purposive incentives.

Material Incentives

In the oft-cited article in which they introduce their three categories of incentives, Wilson and his co-author Peter Clark describe material incentives as "tangible rewards; that is, rewards that have a monetary value or can easily be translated into ones that have" (Clark and Wilson 1961, p. 7). These could be simple monetary payments, but material incentives in the United States have been historically quite diverse.

As we shall see in the next chapter, for example, in the 19th century campaign workers and government employees recognized that their association with their political party provided them with government jobs, and they therefore were willing to provide payments to the party as the price for these material benefits. Considering the number of patronage jobs available, even minimal payments from party loyalists could generate massive party slush funds. In New York City alone, the dominant machine controlled 40,000 jobs in the 1880s (Erie 1988, p. 5). Olson himself points out that the most organizationally dense political party structures are the result of such a system of material benefits and exchange (Olson 1965, p. 164-165).

Material incentives may also come in the form of policy changes provided by lawmakers or regulators that are targeted to increase or maintain one's own welfare. If regulators write a rule in such a way that it singles out a specific contributor's company (or a very few companies of which a contributor's company is one) for special favorable treatment, then this special treatment can be tantamount to a material incentive for giving. Economic theories of regulation call this phenomenon the creation of "inframarginal" or Ricardian rents (McChesney 1997, p. 14). Firms benefit when government policy increases their rivals' relative costs.

Survey data do show that material benefits are a significant consideration, at least to larger contributors. In Francia et al.'s survey of "significant donors," 51 percent say that one factor that is always or sometimes important in their contribution decisions is the fair treatment of their business (Francia et al. 2003, p. 46). If larger contributions generate "access" to politicians, as activists and experts frequently allege (see, e.g. Austen-Smith 1995), then this access may be used as an easy signal that some unspecified (perhaps even unanticipated) material benefit is available to the contributor.

Other material benefits may include the insurance discounts, coupons, and travel deals available to members of such organizations as the AARP and the Sierra Club, or they may even include mugs, t-shirts, bumper stickers, or other such items that are hallmarks of public radio and television funding drives. These small-bore items may not be so intrinsically valuable as to make it rational to contribute from a strict material point of view, but when combined with a particular social significance (prestige – a solidary factor) or a personal sense of satisfaction (a purposive consideration), they may be sufficient to convert a non-contributor into a contributor.

Research on marketing and non-profit fundraising is no stranger to the effectiveness of material incentives as a means to move individuals to action. One guide to non-profit fundraising, for example, points out that "Some organizations offer various premiums for contributions of different sizes. A contribution of $35 may entitle the donor to a coffee mug. Contributions of $120 may entitle the donor to a signed book or a tape of a popular program…[L]apel pins, plaques, certificates, and other tokens of appreciation can be tied to gift club levels" (Weinstein 2009, p. 127)

The above considerations about material incentives allow us to make several straightforward predictions about individual behavior:

> People are more likely to contribute if they have occupations that make a collective good more like a private good.
> People are more likely to contribute if they have received money or gifts from those organizing to provide the collective good.

Material incentives therefore can explain an increased level of individual contributions if people have more directly at stake in political issues being decided, or if organizers and activists offer more money or gifts to contributors.

Solidary Incentives

It is easy to know a material incentive when one sees one: it looks like a gift, a bribe, or another kind of direct personal benefit. The next two types of selective incentives are tougher to identify and measure because they are by their nature more subjective and intangible. The first type of intangible incentive that Clark and Wilson (1961) describe is called "solidary." Such incentives

> derive in the main from the act of associating and include such rewards as socializing, congeniality, the sense of group membership and identification, the status resulting from membership, fun and conviviality, the maintenance of social distinctions, and so on (p. 134-135).

The last fifteen years have seen a boom in scholarship that focuses on so-called "social capital," the good will born of regular meetings and memberships. Authors like Robert Putnam and Theda Skocpol have chronicled the history and geography of group activity in meticulous detail, and have found substantial evidence that membership is related to the incentives that Clark and Wilson described in 1961. Fraternal organizations of the late 19th and early 20th century often reinforced social distinctions, for example (Skocpol 2003). These and other more recent organizations also incorporated ritual, pageantry, and group activities in ways that can only be explained by the fun and conviviality that such practices generated.

Political parties and campaigns are also filled with such rituals. The baby-kissing at the state fair, the colorful campaign signs, and even the wearing of silly hats at national party conventions are all signs that the "hoopla" surrounding modern campaigns continues to draw participants.

In other political science studies, solidary incentives have been linked to the observation that those who are centrally placed in social networks are more likely to participate than those who are not. Much of the research on this subject has been conducted specifically on voting, but as Verba Schlozman and Brady note, the same patterns usually hold for other types of participation as well (Verba, Schlozman, and Brady 1995). As Putnam puts it, "Joiners may be generous souls by nature, but involvement in social networks is a stronger predictor of volunteering and philanthropy than altruistic attitudes per se" (Putnam 2000, p. 121).

One reason that those who are centrally located in social networks are more active is simply that they are easier to reach. Politicians and activists have an easier time discovering those people who have connections, and people who have connections can in turn mobilize others (Rosenstone & Hansen 1993).

From the perspective of the individual, if a person has a connection with someone, that person is more likely to pay attention to his or her requests than if no connection exists. Connections exploit the kinds of social rewards and punishments that Clark and Wilson describe in their definition. As anyone who has used (or invested in) social networking services such as Facebook understands, if a friend asks you to do something, you are more likely to do it, whether it is because you feel guilty about refusing, or whether it means you will have fun doing it, making it less of a burden than it otherwise would be.

Verba, Schlozman, and Brady's incorporation of the social element into their Civic Voluntarism Model makes the idea concrete by suggesting that one reason for non-participation is that "nobody asked me" (Verba, Schlozman, and Brady 1995, p. 16). Recent research on social networks shows that social cues may be much more subtle than a blunt "ask" – in many ways, one's friends behavior conditions one's own behavior (e.g. Fowler and Christakis 2008). The analytical distinction between a solidary incentive and other intangible incentives that can be socially constructed (see the discussion below), is that, as Clark and Wilson say, solidary incentives derive from the act of associating with others. The benefits of social interaction do not occur in isolation – they occur when one affiliates with a group. Such actions might include regular group activities, club meetings, outings, invitations to events, chances to mingle with important people, or other such kinds of associational activity.

Francia et al. find that 26 percent of significant donors say that a contribution's association with "an event I want to attend" is sometimes or always an important reason for giving. Larger percentages admit that a solicitation from "someone I know personally" is a major factor (Francia et al. 2003, p. 46). The solidary incentive here is that one enjoys doing what a friend wants, or, perhaps more accurately, one prefers not to risk a friendship by refusing to do a favor when a friend asks for it.

Indeed, social pressure appears common where solidary incentives are implicated. Married people may have higher voter turnout than single people because one spouse prods the other into voting. A neighborhood or church group may ostracize those who are known to be non-contributors. Gerber, Green, and Larimer have found clear experimental evidence that social pressure affects individuals' decisions on whether to vote or not (Gerber, Green, and Larimer 2008). Professionals in the fields of marketing and philanthropy have used similar insights in their efforts to encourage consumers to buy products or prospective donors to give to charitable causes. Development offices at colleges and universities have worked hard in recent years to build networks of alumni fundraisers to solicit their peers.

A set of predictions about individual behavior deriving from this discussion of solidary incentives is as follows.

> People are more likely to contribute if they enjoy the company of like minded others.
> People are more likely to contribute if they are more embedded within social networks.
> People are more likely to contribute if they have been asked to contribute by someone they know.

Solidary incentives can therefore explain increased numbers of individual contributions if people have a relatively high taste for association, if social networks become more tightly linked for some reason, or if people are more likely to be solicited by members of their social networks.

Internal Incentives

We now move away from the easier, more tangible incentives that can goad a person to action, and enter into a discussion of internal incentives – those incentives that are germane to the individual him or herself and do not concern either material gain or social ties. Because this is the most conceptually difficult of all the incentives delineated here, I spend the most space on this type of motivator.

I begin by outlining the concept of purposive incentives as it was first described by Clark and Wilson, and proceed to a discussion of a later literature that reconceptualizes personal and intangible motivators as "expressive" incentives. These expressive incentives, in turn, can take several different forms, depending on whether one views them as more closely related to social norms or to emotional responses. For each relevant category of internal incentives, I outline (as above) a set of clear predictions about individual behavior.

Purposive Incentives

As with the other incentives listed above, Clark and Wilson (1961) first coined the term "purposive" in an effort to distinguish between different types of organizations (including parties, interest groups, and even private companies). Certain groups could be distinguished from other groups based on the extent to which they relied on purposive incentives as part of their mobilization strategies. Accordingly, the Clark and Wilson theory (extended in Wilson 1995 [1974]) is not directly focused on the individual level, and is instead couched in terms of what strategies will be successful from the standpoint of an organization.

Still, it is possible to develop a view of what motivates individuals based on what purposive organizational strategies Clark and Wilson view as being the most successful. As in the case of other incentives, what is successful for an interest group organization is also likely to be successful for a candidate, since building a fundraising coalition is, after all, an effort in solving a collective action problem.

Clark and Wilson define purposive incentives as follows:

> they are intangible, but they derive in the main from the stated ends of the association rather than from the simple act of associating. These inducements are to be found in the suprapersonal goals of the organization: the demand for the enactment of certain laws or the adoption of certain practices (which do *not* benefit the members in any direct or tangible way), such as elimination of corruption or inefficiency from public service, beautification of the community, dissemination of information about politics or city life, and so forth. Unlike solidary incentives, purposive incentives are inseparable from the ends being sought (Clark and Wilson 1961, p. 135-136, emphasis in original).

Purposive incentives are therefore bound up in particular ends. A social club, a business, or even many traditional political "machine" organizations would have few or no "suprapersonal" purposes and would therefore not appeal to the purposive motivations of individuals. Machine organizer George Washington Plunkitt famously argued that even a powerful principle such as patriotism could not motivate campaign workers if they were not also rewarded with jobs:

> When we tell them that we can't place them, do you think their patriotism is goin' to last? Not much. They say: What's the use of workin' for your country anyhow? There's nothing in the game (Riordan 1995[1905], p. 9).

Plunkitt's organization clearly saw no advantage to relying on purposive incentives. But Clark and Wilson argue that some groups can use such incentives effectively. Successful purposive organizations, they claim, stress the "intrinsic worth or dignity" of their goals (p. 146) and make a convincing case that their organization is more closely associated with these worthwhile goals than are other organizations. Clear statements of the organization's ends are important, but the organization should not get too specific for risk of alienating potential members (p. 147). Specificity leads to conflict over goals, and this conflict can weaken purposive organizations.

Another key ingredient in an organization's success is "producing among members a sense of accomplishment" (p. 148). Without concrete successes, members may abandon the organization. Because such successes are often hard to come by, organizations develop intermediate goals such as service activities or policy research that can be seen as evidence of progress (p. 148). This element of Clark and Wilson's framework bears some similarities to Olson's model of how collective action works. According to his model, people are more likely to contribute to an organization if they see themselves as being decisive or pivotal. An organizational strategy that attempts to link contributions to accomplishment (even intermediary accomplishment) would seem to be an attempt to multiply the opportunities for each person to feel pivotal.

Instead of stressing the overall goal of addressing the problems of poverty and hunger, for example, relief organizations often emphasize the good that an individual contribution will do. The non-profit relief organization CARE, for example, states its overall mission as "defending dignity, fighting poverty," but on its website it features a very tangible intermediate goal: a photograph of a young girl with the caption "help transform her life for only $1 a day."[1]

This focus on accomplishment can also be connected to Verba, Schlozman, and Brady's (1995) research finding that people contribute more when they feel more efficacious. "Activists told us again and again," they write, "that their participation was founded, at least in part, on a desire to influence what the government does" (p. 391). There are two components to this statement: First, an interest in achieving certain goals, and second, a belief on the part of each activist that he or she is capable of increasing the probability of these goals' accomplishment.

Olson is skeptical that "decisiveness" influences much participation, especially when groups are large. Whatever the nature of the collective good to be provided, a prospective group member "would not contribute towards the contribution of any collective or public good, since his own contribution would be imperceptible" (Olson 1965, p. 64). Basic mathematical calculations would appear to support Olson's conclusions. If millions of people contribute to political organizations, parties, and other associations, can each one of these people really think that he or she is making a difference? Organizational strategies of splitting up large goals into many small ones, combined with people's natural cognitive limitations and the fact that a small contribution of money or effort is a "low-cost, low-benefit decision" make this explanation sound more realistic (Aldrich 1993). And still, Clark and Wilson view "purposive organizations" as naturally weak and unstable. "[F]ewer people are willing to accept organizational purposes as a primary incentive than are willing to accept material or solidary inducements," they admit (Clark and Wilson 1961, p. 151).

There are other reasons to believe that individuals' perceptions of their "decisiveness" may be more generous than Olson thought. For example, Tuck (2008) takes issue with what he calls Olson's "negligibility" claims. In his account, people may reasonably consider it worthwhile to contribute if collective good provision requires the simultaneous action of a number of people. Tuck's claim is that potential contributors may not simply calculate the probability that their action was pivotal, but may incorporate in their analysis their own *desire* to have caused the collective outcome. Tuck encourages analysts to think not only of whether a person's contribution was necessary for the collective outcome to occur, but whether it would have been sufficient – even if it was not necessary (Tuck 2008, pp. 100-103). If so, a reasonable person who wishes to have an impact on the outcome may gain more from contributing than from free riding. This sort of reasoning complements Clark and Wilson's account by building a theoretical foundation behind what they find to be successful organizational strategies.

The Clark and Wilson model of purposive incentives, as applied to individual motivations, might therefore be summed up this way:

People are more likely to contribute if they have strong preferences regarding goals.

People are more likely to contribute to organizations with clearly defined goals.

People are more likely to contribute if they feel they can be influential in the accomplishment of a goal or sub-goal.

The increased number of individual contributions since 2000 might then be explained by the increased *salience* of political issues, better *definition* of party and candidate goals, or increased feelings of *efficacy* on the part of potential contributors.

Expressive Incentives
At times, political scientists use the terms "expressive" and "purposive" interchangeably, but in introducing the concept of "expressive" incentives in 1969, Robert Salisbury made a point of distinguishing this idea from Clark and Wilson's framework (Salisbury 1969). This distinction leads to different expectations about individual contribution patterns, and different hypotheses about the source of recent contribution increases.

Like Clark and Wilson, Salisbury focuses on the dynamics of organizations, and distinguishes groups by whether they focus mostly on material, social, or intangible goods. He rejects the "purposive" characterization of these intangibles, however, in favor of a concept of individual motivation derived from Blau's (1964) theory of "expressive social actions." These actions are disconnected from the instrumental pursuit of goals, and instead derive their utility from the simple act of articulating particular values. As Salisbury puts it, "Whether the expression is instrumentally relevant to the achievement of the values in question is, for the moment, not at issue. The point here is that important benefits are derived from the expression itself" (Salisbury 1969, p. 16).[2]

Also like Clark and Wilson, Salisbury sees organizations that rely on intangible incentives as the least durable types of organizations. They are easily formed, but just as easily destabilized, riven by factions, and undermined by rival groups (pp. 19-20). Individual ties to "expressive" organizations are weak and changing. Because the act of contributing is itself an act that generates utility for the contributor, the success or failure of the organization as a whole is not particularly important to those who support it.[3]

Salisbury is not specific about exactly how expression benefits the person doing the expressing. Are these benefits internal and psychological, are they socially defined, or is there a little bit of both taking place? I leave these questions to later sections. For now, a theory of expressive incentives can be distinguished from a theory of purposive incentives by focusing on the following predictions generated by Salisbury's theory:

People will contribute if the act of contributing provides an intrinsic benefit to them.

People's contributions should not depend on whether they feel (or possess) any causal agency towards the provision of a collective or public good.

A focus on expressive incentives would explain recent contribution increases less in terms of increased feelings of efficacy and more in terms of differences in levels of personal satisfaction for contributors relative to non-contributors. Expressive explanations might suggest that the "satisfaction gap" between contributing and not contributing has grown since 2000, at least among some politically relevant subset of the population. The cause of this satisfaction gap might be socially-defined or psychologically-based, two possibilities I examine next.

Socially Defined Expressive Incentives
It is important to distinguish socially-defined expressive incentives from what most people call "solidary" incentives. Clark and Wilson distinguish "solidary" incentives from their other two categories, and do so for good reasons. As discussed above, they see "solidary organizations," as being dependent on "sociability and 'fun'" rather than on any goal-directed activity (Clark and Wilson 1961, p. 141).

Others have argued that social incentives can be characterized by social pressure rather than by entertainment. Olson discusses this possibility in some detail. Because joiners often pursue "prestige, respect, and friendship," if certain members failed to do their parts, the group "might exclude them, and such measures might be effective" (Olson 1965, p.60). This works best in small groups, Olson argues, since it is difficult to ostracize people who are already at a great distance. Scholars of small town politics have often proposed that social pressure dampens the amount of conflict in these communities, providing the public good of "harmony" – or at least the appearance of harmony (Banfield and Wilson 1963, Mansbridge 1980, also see Bryan 2004).

All this has more to do with solidary incentives than with socially defined expressive incentives, however. Socially-defined expressive incentives have less to do with "fun" or coercion than with the internalization of socially-held values: factors having to do with conceptualizations of morality, duty, and justice.   Socially-defined expressive incentives may be so internalized that, as Olson puts it, "the sense of guilt, or the destruction of self-esteem, that occurs when a person feels he has forsaken his moral code" may be enough to make contributions to a public good less costly than non-contribution (Olson 1965, p. 61). Similarly, Hirschman writes, "individuals who have developed a taste for a public good that has yet to be 'produced' and who attempt to get a 'free ride' by letting others exert themselves on their behalf do not just cheat the community as is implied in the free ride metaphor; *they cheat themselves first of all*" (Hirschman 1982, p. 87, emphasis in original).

It may seem inappropriate to distinguish socially-defined expressive incentives from social (or solidary) coercion. Previous work has indeed blurred the distinction, defining participation in collective good provision as a function of the "normative expectations of reference persons" (Opp 1986; Opp 1989) or of the "normative social control system" exercised by group members (Knoke and Wood 1981). But I believe it is useful to separate the direct influence of peer groups (which is closer to social coercion) and the influence of broader values conveyed by much larger contexts such as the political party, the political culture, and society as a whole. These latter effects are less like coercion and related more closely to the "warm glow" effect posited by economic models of "impure altruism" (Andreoni 1989, 1990).

A sense of morality, duty, and justice is no stranger to political science analyses of collective action situations. One proposed solution to the collective action problem of voting adds a "D" term to the standard cost-benefit equation that represents personal satisfaction derived from "compliance with the ethic of voting," from "affirming allegiance to the political system," from "affirming a partisan preference," or from expressing other related values (Riker & Ordeshook 1968, p. 28). Rational choice scholarship has had an uneasy relationship with such an explanation (Aldrich 1993). Olson himself appears to have considered it and dismissed it as untestable (Olson 1965, p. 61). But without adding such a term it can be difficult to explain voting or other low-cost, low-benefit decisions in "rational" terms.[4]

The socially-defined expressive incentives theory of participation suggests several specific expectations.

People are more likely to contribute the more socialized they are to respect common values associated with the political process and political goals.

People are more likely to contribute to candidates and causes in which basic values are more directly invoked or implicated, and less likely to contribute to candidates and causes that are more remote from basic values.

From the perspective of this theory, a change in contribution patterns such as the one we have witnessed since 2000 might be explained as the result of a significant change in socialization patterns, but is more likely to be the result of changes in the political environment that more directly implicate core values.

Emotionally Defined Expressive Incentives
"It doesn't make any difference whether it's ban the bomb or bomb the bastards," Robert Strauss, Chairman of the Democratic National Committee in the 1970s, once said. "People contribute in response to emotional appeals" (Congressional Quarterly 1971, p. 6). Recent research suggests that Strauss was right. A new and growing literature focuses on the role of emotional reactions to political phenomena, and it seems natural to think that these emotional reactions may be linked to expressive incentives for political participation. The work of neuroscientists has divided emotional responses into functions of at least two different "systems": the disposition system and the surveillance system (Marcus 2002). The surveillance system, in particular, is closely connected with the propensity of individuals to take action in response to threats. Most of the time, for most people, the disposition system governs behavior – rewarding behavior that conforms to existing patterns and known routines. When unexpected stimuli enter the environment, however, the surveillance system (usually associated with fear) takes charge, prompting the individual to gather new information in an effort to identify and assess the threat.

In analyzing of the effect of political advertisements, Brader finds empirical support for the theory that "fear may stimulate action to address the threat or induce withdrawal when the path to resolution is unclear" (Brader 2006, p. 107). Brader also finds that politicians target their emotional appeals to geographic regions and subsections of the population in which theories suggest that these ads will have the largest emotional impacts.

The connection to engagement in collective action ought to be clear. If taking action to address a fear satisfies a biologically-ingrained need, then those who participate in collective action may derive an 'expressive benefit' from doing so.

The distinction between the surveillance and the disposition systems may have implications for the effect of new technology on contributor patterns. As we will see in Chapter 4, most fundraisers say that the main effect of technological change is to improve the efficiency of fundraising – a contributor can react almost instantly to a phone call, email, or advertisement by clicking on a mouse and giving a nominal amount. It is possible that the speed with which contributing can occur these days means that the surveillance system rather than the disposition system is more likely to be in play when the potential contributor makes his or her decision. In any case, a theory of emotionally defined expressive incentives leads to the following prediction.

> People who are affectively engaged with politics – particularly those whom politics makes more fearful – will be more likely to contribute.

Emotional factors might be linked to the recent rise in contributions because of candidates' and parties' increasing facility with using dire warnings and other scare tactics about the consequences of electing rival candidates and parties to office. The 2008 election was full of such warnings, which spilled over into issues such as the 2009 debates over fiscal policy and health care reform. The increased capacity of the internet to spread unfounded rumors and bitter invective may also have contributed to increased fears and increased contributions since 2000. Finally, the widely documented polarization of the political parties may have made the consequences of a victory by the opposing party seem more dire to potential contributors. When the alternative candidate is farther away from one's own position, that candidate may seem "scarier."

Conclusion

This chapter has considered at least four (and probably five) distinct theoretical bases for contributing to a collective good. Most of the theories outlined above were originally designed to explain interest group formation and dissolution, but they can easily be considered within the context of campaign fundraising because candidates – like interest group leaders are faced with collective action problems.

I have discussed each theory separately in the interest of clarity. This distinct discussion of each theory will also be useful in the next two chapters, when I move on to test these theories using two key datasets. There is nothing that prevents multiple motives from operating at the same time within the same individuals, however. On the contrary, it would be surprising to find anything else. Interest groups, as scholars at least since Clark and Wilson have acknowledged, use a variety of different strategies for organization, a fact that not only suggests that different participants may have different motives, but that also raises the possibility that people have multiple motives for contributing. An additional – and distinct – possibility is that these motives are not additive, but multiplicative; having two motives may make one more than twice as likely to contribute, for example. The question of why people give to campaigns and causes may have more than one clear answer.

---

[1] www.care.org, accessed August 6, 2012.

[2] Also see Terry Moe (1980) on the difference between an individual's "evaluation of collective goods" versus a person's "purposive sense of satisfaction from the act of contributing itself." It is this latter motive that Salisbury refers to as "expressive".

[3] Schuessler (2000) links expressive incentives to organizational and electoral success by arguing that individuals are motivated by the ability to claim responsibility for desirable outcomes. But it would seem that even by this logic, success or failure is not crucial. Witness the popularity of bumper stickers along the lines of "Don't Blame Me: I voted for McCain."

[4] A theory of socially-defined expressive incentives also bears a resemblance to some economic models of altruistic behavior. See, for example, Becker 1976.

3

The History of U.S. Campaign Finance

The discussion in Chapter 2 shows that there are at least five main ways to view individuals' decisions about whether or not to give money to political candidates and causes. They may give for material reasons, for social reasons, or for one of three types of "intangible" purposive or expressive reasons. People may also give for multiple reasons, meaning that each individual contribution might have more than one cause. The remainder of this book moves from the theoretical world to the empirical one, in an effort to investigate which of these explanations has the most support in the experience of U.S. campaign giving. If we can focus on several "most likely" reasons for giving, we draw nearer to an explanation of how individual contribution patterns shape the campaign finance system.

In this chapter, I offer a historical account of campaign finance patterns. I begin with a brief history of campaign financing in the U.S. form the late 1800s to the present day. One theme that emerges from this examination of history is that political fundraising has evolved as a profession that is closely related to the business of marketing and to the practice of philanthropic giving. Previous literature has rarely placed campaign giving in the context of marketing and philanthropy, but when one of these fields makes a technological or strategic advance, it quickly migrates to the other two.

This close relationship is due to the fact that both marketing and philanthropy must grapple with problems that are similar to raising money for politics. As discussed above, the key puzzle in modern campaign finance is why so many people contribute to campaigns and causes. In the case of philanthropy, the similarities should be obvious in light of the discussion in the previous two chapters: Why contribute to a charitable cause if one gets no personal benefit, and if an individual contribution is a "drop in the bucket" in light of the overall problem? The vast majority of philanthropic giving in the United States comes from individuals rather than foundations, and comes in small amounts rather than large chunks (Lindahl 2010, p. 10; Frumkin 2006, p. 4). No wonder students of philanthropy see the question of why people give as among the most important to their field.

The case of marketing may seem less similar to campaign finance, since it relates to the private sector economy and therefore deals in private, rather than public goods. If a customer purchases a product, he or she benefits by having that product. Consumer choices are not always simple, however. As one marketing text puts it, "Customers do not come to each buying decision with conveniently blank minds, and then rationally consider the options" (Mercer 1996, p. 51-52). The job of marketers is to delve into the complexities of consumer choice, deciphering the often contradictory impulses that affect purchasing. The most successful marketing strategies can convince people they need something that they did not think they needed prior to being contacted.

If people respond to political appeals for reasons that are related to why they respond to philanthropic and commercial appeals, this broadens the amount of evidence that can be brought to bear on the phenomenon of campaign donations. Even if political donors are different from other donors, these differences can teach us about each type of contribution.

The historical record on campaign fundraising also brings to light clear continuities between the present and the past. Fundraisers have not always employed the same strategies or the same technology, but a finance director on a 2012 presidential campaign would recognize the same principles of fundraising at work a century earlier. Because of these continuities, we can learn more than we might expect about modern fundraising by paying attention to the campaigns of decades past. It has never been an easy matter to sustain a campaign on small individual donations. But there have always been at least some candidates who inspire floods of donations in small amounts from enthusiastic supporters.

To conclude the chapter, I briefly examine aggregate data on political giving over the past 30 years – the period for which the best data are available. These data allow us to see how individual contributions have (and have not) changed as the campaign finance environment has changed. As I indicate in the introduction, the number of individual contributions has soared, and candidates may have become more sophisticated in differentiating their strategies in recent years. But many core features of fundraising remain the same. Large donors have not gone away as small donors have increased in number, for example. Nor have PACs vanished from the campaign finance scene.

Individual Contributions in U.S. Politics: A Brief History

Getting elected to office in the United States has never been cheap or easy. The earliest political candidates were expected to fund their own campaigns. Many histories of campaign finance begin with a reference to George Washington's successful 1758 campaign for a seat in the Virginia House of Burgesses, in which he "opened accounts with four taverns in Winchester to provide impressive quantities of rum, wine, and beer at the polls" (Ellis 2004, p. 36). This extravagance cost far less than it would today, since the total number of voters was below 800.

As the modern political party system developed during and after the 1820s, campaigns became more expensive as more voters entered the electorate. The chief contributors to the parties were initially not ordinary voters, however – they were those who materially benefited from the party organizations.

Beginning with the Jacksonian "spoils system," parties developed a symbiotic patronage-based relationship with their supporters. The party provided its campaign workers with jobs, and these supporters in turn provided the party with funds. These kickbacks (known as "assessments") typically amounted to between one and two percent of a worker's overall salary.[1] As political scientist Louise Overacker put it in 1932, "Sometimes men give to get jobs and sometimes they give to keep them" (Overacker 1932, p. 169). The system – very clearly based on the exchange of material benefits – provided grist for editorial cartoons and partisan sniping, but did not become a central point of controversy for decades, perhaps because the amounts spent on campaigns were not staggering, nor was the staff of the federal government very large. Writing in 1926, political scientist James Pollock made the nostalgic observation that "Back in the [eighteen]'sixties, when very modest campaign funds were utilized by the political parties, it was not very important to know how the money was raised or whence it came" (Pollock 1926, p. 62).

As the amount of money spent in national campaigns increased in the latter part of the 19th century, civil service reformers became much more strident in their criticisms of the assessment system. Policy changes followed, although not all of these reforms were effective. President Rutherford Hayes signed an executive order in 1877 declaring with authority that "no assessments for political purposes upon officers or subordinates will be allowed." He then promptly approved a plan to distribute to employees a series of "Government printed circulars" that "suggested" specific donations to the Republican Party for its 1878 races.[2]

The 1883 Pendleton Act, which created a merit civil service, was more successful in curbing the assessment system. Some stalwarts protested, but by the late 1880s, fundraisers resigned themselves to the new environment and turned increasingly away from assessments on public workers and politicians for their funding. This transition from assessments to private giving meant that party fundraisers were now faced with the task of convincing people to voluntarily give them money – a more difficult matter than simply taking a cut of dependent party loyalists' salaries. Although most contributors at this time were the very wealthy, they were not always easy to solicit – party officials often complained about how little they were able to extract from businessmen who they thought ought to sympathize with their causes (Summers 2002). To cope with this difficulty, innovative partisans began to lay the foundations for some of the later techniques that would broaden the contributor pool considerably.

It is this turn from patronage-based fundraising to fundraising from voluntary contributions that marks the transition to a system quite similar in its basic characteristics to the system we live in today. Party leaders faced an obvious collective action problem. Even sympathetic potential contributors had little incentive to donate to the collective cause in the absence of separate selective incentives. Bureaucrats that could be hired and fired were easy to coerce; political party leaders had less sway over the captains of industry. By the 1880s, therefore, party fundraisers had begun a dedicated search for methods of solving this collective action problem. They found some important clues in the related, but distinct, fields of marketing and philanthropic giving.

The 1888 race was a particular turning point, and provides an early example of how marketing, philanthropy, and fundraising have come together in politics. Appointed as Republican National Committee (RNC) chair because of his connections and fundraising prowess, Pennsylvania Senator (and state party boss) Matthew Quay orchestrated a large scale effort to raise money from wealthy contributors for the campaign of Benjamin Harrison (Kehl 1981, p. 97). To manage the effort, Quay relied not on his own experience with patronage in Philadelphia (as he might have in the earlier era of assessments), but on the business skills of Philadelphia merchant, philanthropist, and marketing pioneer John Wanamaker.

Wanamaker had built his career by developing a marketing strategy based on frank and direct communication with consumers. As described by his advertising manager, "the Wanamaker Advertising Idea" was grounded in scrupulous honesty about a product's merits and, if necessary, drawbacks. "Even if [an advertisement] is crude in form, awkward in expression, ragged in get-up, so there's a streak of honest thought and good intent running through it, all else is overlooked."[3] Offering customers a "money-back guarantee" gave shoppers further confidence in Wanamaker's claims. As his adoring biographer Joseph Appel put it, "The fundamental purpose of Wanamaker advertising may be summed up in nine words: 'Not to sell, but to help people to buy'" (Appel 1930, p. 397). Later generations of marketers would return to this point about the importance of fostering and maintaining consumer trust.

Thrust into the world of political fundraising, Wanamaker set about his task by insisting on installing an advisory committee of businessmen at the RNC, each of whom would assist in soliciting contributors. As he later recalled, "I had a large experience in raising money, from my connection with the Christian Association and other enterprises of that sort. If you have a large purpose and can bring it to bear on large-minded men, you may as well ask for ten thousand dollars as for five hundred dollars, for men are rather complemented when you ask them higher, and they sacrifice high for a worthy end."[4]

Wanamaker and his committee proved to be disciplined and successful fundraisers. His experience in business and charity (as a leader of the Christian Commission, founded during the Civil War to provide spiritual and social guidance for soldiers), led Wanamaker to understand how to match a lofty cause with a frank and earnest marketing campaign. His coordinated, efficient fundraising operation took the opposite party by surprise and, in Wanamaker's view, won the campaign before the other party had a chance to get started. "[The Democrats] had their spies out, supposing that we were going to do something," Wanamaker later recalled, "but before they knew what it was, we had them beaten. They were not beaten in November or in October, but long before that."[5] The newly-elected President Harrison was uncomfortable with patronage generally, but he had no trouble appointing Wanamaker to be Postmaster General.

Wanamaker's fundraising efforts addressed the collective action problem from multiple angles at once. He and his committee worked through existing social networks so that social pressures (solidary incentives) might reinforce solicitations for funds. They made ideological appeals to call on the higher angels of their prospects' natures (purposive or expressive incentives). And they drew on the frank and open Wanamaker marketing philosophy to establish and maintain trust between themselves and their potential contributors. On its own, each of these methods might have fallen short. Together, they allowed the Republicans to build a solid and successful fundraising operation.

The 1890s saw centralized, professionalized fundraising efforts by the national parties come into full flower as fundraisers from both parties adopted and expanded upon the Wanamaker model. During this period the parties focused on expanding the pool of wealthy elite donors as widely as possible, innovating here and there, but largely building on Wanamaker's tactics. Humiliated by their 1888 defeat, Democrats responded in 1892 with an unprecedented effort of their own, led by the wealthy and well-connected New Yorker William Whitney (Pollock 1926, p. 63). As if to punctuate his determination, Whitney personally contributed $20,000, doubling Wanamaker's donation to his party four years before (Graff 2008, p. 69).

The rise of Republican mastermind Mark Hanna put all previous party financing efforts to shame. As chief advisor to Ohio Governor William McKinley, Hanna was a natural choice to head the RNC after McKinley became the party's 1896 nominee. Pitted against the eloquent and youthful Democrat William Jennings Bryan, Republicans sought to compensate by orchestrating a national publicity campaign, flooding the country with pamphlets, flyers, leaflets, and pre-written newspaper columns for local papers to print (Croly 1912, p. 217-218). This was expensive, so Hanna set himself to the task of raising more money than had ever before been raised in an American presidential race. If part of Wanamaker's appeal to prospective donors had been to principle, Hanna's pitch was more closely connected to self-interest. He aggressively pressed inflation-averse east coast business and financial interests to make large contributions to forestall Bryan's efforts to freely coin silver (Horner 2010, p. 194). The Standard Oil Company alone gave $250,000 (Croly 1912, p. 220). Definitive records do not exist, but it seems clear that the 1896 Republican effort cost at least $3.5 million, many times what Democrats were able to raise and spend. Three million dollars came from donors in the state of New York alone (Croly 1912, p. 200).

The old system of assessments had given way to a professionalized system of raising money from elites whose interests aligned with those of the political parties involved. As historian Herbert Croly wrote of the 1896 race, "The Republican Party became the representative of the interests and needs of American business, and inevitably American business men came liberally to its support" (Croly 1912, p. 222). Economic interests of a different sort – western and southern agrarian interests – supported Bryan's silverism, but their resources were no match for New York's.

Large contributions of this sort are more easily explained from a collective action framework than the smaller contributions that funded Bryan. Each mega-donor might have presumed that his business's interests would be protected by the new administration, so material incentives could have played a major role. Those who contributed generously could often claim a plumb appointment in a new administration. Out of seventeen people who contributed more than $10,000 to Woodrow Wilson's presidential campaign, eight received jobs in the Wilson administration (Overacker 1932, p. 171).

Furthermore, in the case of individuals who contributed tens of thousands of dollars – and certainly in the case of whole companies that contributed hundreds of thousands – each contributor might plausibly have considered himself (or, much more rarely during this period, herself) as being a pivotal part of the campaign's efforts. This was even more likely to be true for those who gave generously to elect members of Congress. Philadelphia industrialist Albert M. Greenfield contributed more than a quarter of the total fund for William Vare's 1926 race for the Republican Senate nomination in Pennsylvania, for example (Overacker 1932, pp. 120-121).

Whether the reason was to advance their policy aims or to receive material benefits, the wealthy had good reason to be involved in politics in the first decades of the 20th century. Those who see U.S. party politics as a clash between moneyed factions in which voters have little agency can make quite a convincing case about the late 19th and early 20th centuries (Ferguson 1995).

Just as the party fundraising operations were becoming increasingly expert at raising money from sympathetic business interests, however, a change was afoot. The three presidential races following 1896 were much less competitive, causing the parties to pull back from the aggressive solicitation that had defined their most intense contests. More importantly, in 1907 Congress enacted the Tillman Act, which prohibited corporate contributions to federal campaigns. At the time the new law (which is still in place) had no clear enforcement mechanism, so it might have been possible for the parties to simply ignore it. Undoubtedly, substantial corporate money made its way into politics despite the legal change. Nevertheless, the reform represented a clear signal that voters had grown uncomfortable with the domination of campaign finance by wealthy interests. In response to the anti-corporate mood, both parties declared they would be more transparent in their raising and spending of campaign money (Pollock 1926, p. 67).

One way to complement this transparency was to seek to broaden the fundraising base, moving from a system dominated by wealthy contributors to one in which there was more balance between elites and average voters. This represented good public relations, and it held out the promise of reinforcing enthusiasm among party regulars, who might see themselves as part of a larger cause, in the same way Wanamaker had promised his wealthier donors they would be. In the 1920s, both parties experimented with raising money from much larger pools of contributors than they had in the past.

Party leaders were encouraged in these efforts by the example of William Jennings Bryan's presidential campaigns, which had, especially in 1908, stressed the importance of small contributions and transparent fundraising (Hibben 1929, p. 285). Political operatives cannot have failed to notice that, although Bryan fell short of raising as much money as his Republican opponents, he had been very successful at raising money in smaller amounts. Perhaps not coincidentally, his followers were passionate and devoted. The typical Bryan campaign events were "like the swinging of a firebrand in a powder mill," with ecstatic admirers crowding many campaign stops (Morgan 1969, p. 512). Could other campaigns reproduce the enthusiasm of Bryan's followers by emphasizing small contributions? Top fundraisers in both parties were willing to give it a try.

The 1920 presidential race saw the first coordinated effort to change fundraising from (solely) a matter of raising cash to a matter of extending the party's pool of committed supporters. After the election of 1916 left the Democratic National Committee swamped with debt, the party looked to its director of finance, William Jamieson, to help build a more solid financial foundation. Jamieson proposed a novel strategy. Raising money, he suggested, was not just about funding campaign expenses. Jamieson suggested that, as the Bryan campaigns had shown, raising cash could also be about cultivating a broad and enthusiastic base of support. He proposed building a massive nationwide list of up to four million people, of whom perhaps one million (he hoped) would become contributors. As Jamieson put it later in congressional testimony,

> My idea was this…That, of course, I wanted the Democrats to win this year, and I thought the best thing I could do to help them win would be to get just as many contributors as possible to the campaign fund. I was not thinking about the amount. I was thinking about this fact: That the person – the voter – who makes a contribution to your campaign is apt to be a good worker in your campaign (Kenyon Committee 1921, p. 1560).

Jamieson's insight was that even if a minimal amount of money could be raised in tiny increments, such a fundraising effort would still be worthwhile because it would also reinforce the party's support, and might elevate that support to the level of a moral commitment. As Jamieson put it, "Every man ought to contribute the same as he would from a religious motive. We don't want any money from anyone who figures he is making an investment."[6] Here Jamieson was expressly rejecting appeals to material incentives in favor of an appeal to intangible incentives. Specifically, according to the framework outlined in Chapter 2, Jamieson was appealing to an expressive incentive. What was more, he believed that a single expressive behavior (a contribution) would be likely to lead to further expressive behavior (campaign work).

Many modern campaigns would recognize the Jamieson idea in their own strategic fundraising plans. The process of fundraising allows a candidate to reach out to supporters; the process of contributing helps make supporters more enthusiastic about the candidate. Contributions and solicitations can help build the bonds of trust between candidates and supporters in the same way that John Wanamaker's frank and honest ads had build a bond of trust between his company and customers. In the same way that Wanamaker's approach represented an early vision of where marketing and philanthropic understandings of campaign fundraising would go in the ensuing century, the Jamieson plan recognized an aspect of campaign finance similar to what marketers were learning around the same time. Successful marketing is about building productive relationships with customers, thereby improving the probability of repeat business. An Obama campaign official made this same point in 2011: "[A contribution is] not just a contribution — making a small dollar contribution to the campaign increases the likelihood that that person will volunteer, it increases the likelihood that they will engage their networks on the president's behalf, and it increases the likelihood that they will give again."[7] As Jennifer Steen has suggested, candidates that finance their campaigns out of their own personal wealth may sacrifice this important aspect of fundraising (Steen 2006).

Jamieson's grand ambitions in the 1920 campaign were not realized, however. By September his plan had fallen short of expectations, and the party abandoned its extensive mailing lists in favor of a more traditional method of appointing local finance directors and having them "pass the hat among their office-holding friends and those who may be hoping for future favors from those in control of the national party organization."[8] So much for not wanting contributions from anyone who "figures he is making an investment."

Republicans that same year tried a hybrid strategy, adopting a solicitation method "substantially the same as that used by the Red Cross and by the Liberty Loan organizations in their drives" during World War I (Pollock 1926, p. 71). The party established a series of committees at the national and state level, each of which was put in charge of collecting contributions while simultaneously spreading the party message. This resulted in a significant number of very small contributions. In the state of Michigan, for example, the party collected about $170,000 from 2,115 contributors – three quarters of whom gave $50 or less – still a substantial sum in those days, but not an outlandish amount. Over 350 people contributed just one dollar (Pollock 1926, p. 76). "Upon the acquainting of the party public of the purpose depended the success of the undertaking," RNC Chairman Will Hays said later, "and upon the publicity depended the political interest, which was just as much our objective as the contributions" (Kenyon Committee 1921, p. 1082). Hays acknowledged the possibility that fundraising would generate enthusiasm, just as Jamieson had, but he hedged his bets by maintaining its large-donor base.

As the Jamieson plan's mixed results – and the Republican hybrid strategy's greater degree of success – show, it was difficult if not impossible during this period to fund a successful nationwide campaign on the basis of small contributions alone. Instead, small contributions provided a useful and productive supplement to the funds donated by larger contributors.

This point proved to be true not only of the 1920s, but of campaign finance for the next century. As political scientist Frank Sorauf puts it, "attempts to raise substantial sums from small contributors rarely made the big contributors superfluous in national politics" (Sorauf 1992, p. 3). As a case in point, in 1928 the national committees spent a total of $7.2 million on the election, much of which continued to come from wealthy Americans (Overacker 1932, p. 80). A significant minority of campaigns did rely disproportionately on small contributors, but these campaigns tended to be led by insurgents: Roosevelt's Bull Moosers in 1912; LaFollette's Progressives in 1924; and Socialists in various campaigns during the same era (Overacker 1932, p. 110). Certain campaigns could rely on small contributors, therefore, but typical campaigns could not.

Parties continued to be the primary gatherers of campaign cash into the early post-World War II period, although candidates for House and Senate were increasingly likely to rely on their personal organizations and resources (Parker 2008). In the 1950s, candidates for Congress and the presidency grew increasingly independent of the party organizations. Not coincidentally, around this same time marketing and public relations professionals took on a greater role in political campaigns. These firms facilitated the divergence of candidates from parties by providing individual campaigns with the kinds of services that the parties used to supply.

Husband and wife team Clem Whitaker and Leone Baxter started the first full-service political consultancy, Campaigns Inc., in 1933, taking advantage of their skills in the worlds of business and public relations. They were a full service consultancy, but fundraising and budgeting were key aspects of the advice they gave candidates. As previous successful fundraisers had done, they modeled their campaign strategy on a marketing and business approach. "We do our utmost, in every campaign," said Whitaker, "to get a dollar's value for every dollar spent, just as if we were merchandising *commodities* instead of selling *men* and *measures*" (Kelley 1956 p. 39). The firm developed an intricate, well-organized and targeted fundraising strategy, which tailored its appeals to demographic, social, and geographic categories of people (Baker 2002). Whitaker and Baxter achieved early success in California, in part because their skills were sorely needed in a state without strong party organizations, but their techniques soon spread to other firms in other states.

New laws continued to tighten regulation of campaign finance, and to require regular disclosure of fundraising totals, but the lack of enforcement makes it difficult for contemporary researchers to be certain about broad patterns of congressional fundraising. The 1907 ban on corporate and bank contributions to campaigns was followed by a new disclosure law (in 1911), spending limits for congressional races (in 1925), and contribution limits (in 1940), but these laws were largely ineffectual in controlling campaign expenditures or tracking spending. Although each Congressional candidate's principal campaign committee was required to report to the clerk of the House or the Secretary of the Senate, for example, this did not preclude campaigns from establishing multiple committees. A single committee's contributions and expenditures might be disclosed, but there would be unknown other committees spending and fundraising without full reporting. Today, although reporting records from this period are available in Congressional files, the Secretary of the Senate's office cautions researchers against drawing any substantive conclusions from them.

Political scientists Alexander Heard and Herbert Alexander conducted the best available studies of money and politics in the 1960s, and offer selective data on congressional campaigns during this period. Studies of Senate candidates in Tennessee and California show that, in these states at least, candidates relied primarily on larger donors and did not make "serious efforts to collect contributions from small givers" (Owens 1970, p. 52). As one candid fundraiser described the process of raising money in California, "you have to understand what interests contributors, what they want – power, position or prestige or some kind of service from government – and use this knowledge as a lever to raise funds" (Owens 1970, p. 51). This is a clear assertion that material incentives were the most important inducement for campaign contributions.

Presidential campaigns followed a similar pattern to that of the 1920s and 1930s, although the sums involved and the technologies used to raise them did evolve. Republican Barry Goldwater (in 1964) and Democrat George McGovern (in 1972) performed particularly well in raising funds from small contributors. As in the case of William Jennings Bryan, these small-donor successes appear to have been due to a combination of grassroots enthusiasm and lack of alternative funding sources. Shunned by larger business donors early in the 1964 campaign, Goldwater and his staff publicized a national effort to gather money in smaller amounts. As a result, nearly 700,000 people contributed to his campaign in an era when other presidential campaigns had no more than a few tens of thousands of contributors (Alexander 1966 p. 70). Eight years later, McGovern nearly equaled Goldwater's number of contributors, relying on a direct mail campaign known as the "Million Member Club" (Alexander 1976).[9]

Goldwater and McGovern – like Robert LaFollette or William Jennings Bryan in earlier decades – led enthusiastic movement-like groups of supporters who were committed to the causes they advocated. Other measures of passionate commitment – such as the numbers of grassroots volunteers each campaign recruited – support this assessment. Like LaFollette and Bryan, Goldwater and McGovern lost their elections, however, overwhelmed by their better financed and (perhaps more importantly) more politically savvy and broadly popular opponents. Those with an enthusiastic small-donor base seemed to have only narrow appeal to the electorate at large.

The technology of making appeals to potential contributors continued to advance in the 1960s and 1970s. Scholars often point to this era as a pivotal period in incorporating the tools of marketing into politics, an observation that is in no small part due to Joe McGinniss's classic book *The Selling of the President, 1968*. McGinniss's cynical perspective on the subject continues to resonate today. "Politics, in a sense, has always been a con game," wrote McGinniss.

...Advertising, in many ways, is a con game, too. Human beings do not need new automobiles every third year; a color television set brings little enrichment of the human experience; a higher or lower hemline no expansion of consciousness, no increase in the capacity to love.

It is not surprising then, that politicians and advertising men should have discovered one another. And, once they recognized that the citizen did not so much vote for a candidate as make a psychological purchase of him, not surprising that they began to work together (McGinniss 1969, p. 26-27).

McGinniss's gripping account of Nixon's "advertising men" made it seem as if the 1968 campaign was the dawn of something entirely new. It is probably more accurate to say that the 1950s and 1960s saw major developments in marketing and fund-raising generally, and that it was only a matter of time before these innovations spread over into politics. As we have seen, marketing and fundraising have always cross-pollinated with political campaigns. As early as 1920, Albert Lasker of the Lord and Thomas Advertising Agency helped Warren Harding in his campaign against Jamieson's Democrats by coining such memorable phrases as "Let's Have Done with Wiggle and Wobble" (Casey 1935, p. 104).

By the late 1950s, public relations firms often had so-called "political accounts" and state party committees frequently employed public relations firms.[10] The relative decline of political parties in the realm of campaign finance and the parallel rise of television made it all the more likely that politicians and marketers would "discover one another." The 1960 campaign, in which John Kennedy's dynamic and youthful image seemed inseparable from his success, accelerated the scramble for the services of the new political consultants (Newman 1999, p. 22).

Consultants, advertising specialists, and other professionals were all increasingly central to campaign management and organization. But the crucial technological innovation from a fundraising perspective arose from the field of marketing. This was the "direct mail" technique, a method that greatly increased the efficiency of fundraising appeals. Direct mail itself had been around for decades: it had been developed in the 1880s and 1890s by Sears Roebuck. Advances in technology and the organization of data had made the technique cheaper, quicker, and easier to target, however, and soon political activists began recognizing the potential of the tactic for political purposes.

One of the earliest political direct mailers was Richard Viguerie, who made his name fundraising for the conservative organization Young Americans for Freedom in the late 1960s. Viguerie built a marketing conglomerate from the humble beginnings of a list of conservative donors painstakingly compiled from the names of those who had made small contributions to the Goldwater campaign in 1964. Conservatives, he reasoned, had plenty of intellectual firepower, "But I realized that what we [conservatives] didn't have was someone who could take the ideas, the writings, and the books, and market them to the people....So I set out to become the best marketer I could be. I determined to learn how to successfully market ideas to millions" (Armstrong 1988, p. 44). Viguerie's biographical statement at his current website, conservativeHQ.com, claims that his development of direct mail "transformed American politics in the 1960s and 1970s."[11] Viguerie is one of the few people who can plausibly make such a sweeping claim.

Conservatives at first did much better with list-gathering and direct-mail marketing than did liberals, but candidates and party organizations from all sides of the spectrum ultimately took advantage of the computerized direct-mail political marketing that Viguerie helped develop. George McGovern's 1972 presidential campaign was so successful at raising money from a large base of donors because the candidate himself had recognized the importance of building a comprehensive direct mail list as early as 1969 (Armstrong 1988, p. 52). McGovern even announced his candidacy by mail in a move that generated the same swell of excitement among activists as Barack Obama's 2008 announcement of his Vice Presidential choice via text message. The McGovern announcement mailing generated ten times the amount of money it cost to produce (Armstrong 1988, p. 55).

As direct mail consultants perfected their craft, they developed a better understanding of how emotion played a role in their success. Although marketing in general is influenced by considerations of emotion, the technique of direct mail marketing seemed particularly able to tap into key emotions that could motivate action. First, direct mail established a relationship between the solicitor and the potential contributor, a fundamental fact of which marketers are perennially aware. If this relationship can be infused with a degree of trust – if the contributor believes that the organization has his or her best interests in mind – then the job of the direct mail marketer becomes easier. There are numerous ways to establish this trust, but the most common is to associate the appeal with a well known personality – the candidate, perhaps, but also the candidate's spouse, a local sports hero, or a well known and well-loved figure in the party.

Second, direct mail professionals found that many contributors donate for starkly emotional reasons. According to one consultant, the four key reasons a person gives money are "exclusivity," "greed," "guilt," and "fear" (Armstrong 1988, p. 49). Expert practitioners report that fear or anger are particularly strong motivators. McGovern's supporters feared a continuing war in Vietnam. Goldwater supporters worried about the destruction of individual liberties and states' rights. As the examples above in Chapter 1 show, groups such as Planned Parenthood, the American Civil Liberties Union, and the NRA benefit from a surge of contributions when their core interests appear to be threatened.

In the late 1960s and 1970s, new interest groups and more technologically-savvy candidates drew heavily on such techniques. Hedrick Smith's classic book *The Power Game* describes Tim Wirth, a Colorado congressman in the 1970s and 1980s, as having assiduously cultivated a list of "150,000 names, broken down into one thousand different categories" (Smith 1996 [1988], p. 149). Members of each category of people would presumably receive letters focused on the issues of most import to them. Not all of this effort was devoted to fundraising – most mail simply helped the member of Congress keep in touch with constituents and convince them that their representative cared about the same issues they did.

In the early 1970s, the campaign finance regime changed as Congress enacted new reforms in the wake of the Watergate scandals (some of which involved campaign finance abuses). The Federal Election Commission, which writes regulations and archives data; the presidential public financing system; and an effective set of contribution limits all date back to the 1974 Federal Election Campaign Act amendments (usually referred to simply as "FECA"). (Congress also enacted spending limits for congressional races, but the Supreme Court struck these down as an encroachment on free speech in the landmark 1976 case of *Buckley* v. *Valeo*.) This new system forced candidates to be more fastidious in their data collection and reporting, although contributions amounting to less than $200 did not (and do not) have to be itemized individually. The previous system of multiple campaign committees also became untenable, so from the 1970s forward, we can be quite confident that campaigns spent more or less what they say they spent.

One notable effect of contribution limits was to encourage a somewhat broader base of contributors by capping the amounts that a candidate's core group of wealthiest supporters could give. As one fundraiser put it, "Used to be, you'd get a dozen people in the room and come up with half a million dollars for sure. Now if you get $25,000 you're doing great" (Brown, Powell, & Wilcox 1995, p. 19). Candidates had to respond by broadening their support base, raising money earlier, and spending more of their personal time on the phone with prospective donors.

At the time, the contribution caps of $1,000 per person may have had more effect on presidential races than on congressional races, since the number of contributors willing and capable of donating $1,000 per campaign, per election (or $2,000 per election cycle, since the primary and general elections count separately) was small. Until 2002, however, this contribution limit did not increase to account for inflation, meaning that more and more contributors were capable of bumping up against the limits. Today, campaigns must be mindful of how much "capacity" remains with their wealthy core contributors. During the 2008 primary race, for example, Hillary Clinton's staff fretted that many of their major donors had already "maxed out." Similar grumblings took place in 2012 among Republicans concerned that Mitt Romney's campaign had rapidly reached its maximum "get" from many of its core contributors.[12]

Another effect of the reforms was to give rise to Political Action Committees as a major source of funds for congressional campaigns. These groups, formed for the express purpose of taking part in political activity, can be "separate segregated funds" linked to business and labor organizations, or they may be independent of any other organization. Technically, PACs had existed for decades – they had been an innovation of the Congress of Industrial Organizations (CIO) in the 1940s (Corrado, et al. 1997, p. 30). But the new law encouraged these groups in an effort to make the interests associated with campaigns more readily identifiable. Predictably, PACs became an easy target for reform groups in the 1980s and 1990s. Amid the many reform proposals circulating in Congress during this time were innumerable plans to ban or severely restrict PACs (Dwyre & Farrar-Myers, 2001).

By 2000, candidates had a broad range of fundraising options in a number of different categories. The 1970s reforms had forced them to somewhat extend their use of mass-marketing techniques. But for the most part, campaigns rely on political action committees and wealthy contributors capable of handing over $1000 or more as their primary source of funds. Former Senator Bill Bradley describes the trade-offs well in his 1996 memoir:

> Occasionally, a politician will raise money through direct-mail solicitation aimed at targeted mailing lists. This approach yields many small contributions, but it takes time and a big investment up front. If

Figure 3.1: Total Cost of Political Campaigns vs. GDP Growth, 1960-2008

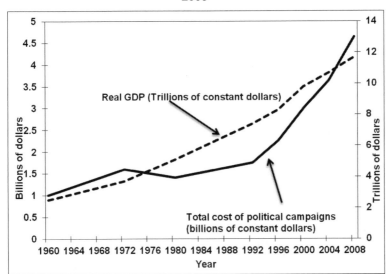

Source: Federal Election Commission, OpenSecrets.org, Bureau of Economic Analysis.

3 percent of those mailed to actually respond, the mailing is considered a success. Once someone contributes, you can probably get that person to contribute a second or third time during the campaign, but, as with compound interest, it takes time before big money builds up. ...Usually,...the financial base of federal legislators comes from PACs and the rich (Bradley 1996, p. 177).

In the dozen years since the turn of the century, rapid changes in the campaign environment have held out the possibility of transforming political campaigns. New laws such as the 2002 Bipartisan Campaign Reform Act (BCRA or "McCain-Feingold") have increased the amounts individuals can contribute to candidates, while restricting the ability of political parties to raise money in large chunks from so-called "soft money" contributors. The Supreme Court's 2010 decision in *Citizens United* v. *FEC* opened the door for corporate and union spending in elections, and also paved the way for "Super PACs" that can collect unlimited amounts from individual contributors as long as the PACs themselves do not directly contribute to candidates.

Figure 3.2: Charitable Giving as a Percent of GDP, 1970-2010

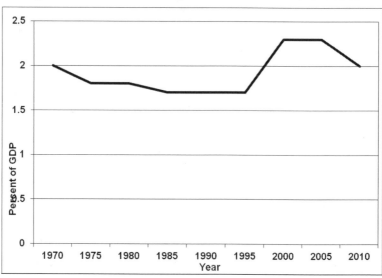

Source: Giving USA 2011, Giving USA Foundation.

New technologies such as email, websites, social networking, and "microtargeting" techniques have changed the tools that fundraisers have at their disposal. As I show in the next chapter, professional fundraisers themselves disagree about the extent to which the terrain of political giving has changed in the last decade. In many cases, campaigns raise money the old fashioned way: by putting the candidate on the phone and giving him or her a list of prospects to call. On the other hand, there are cases like the Ron Paul campaign and the Barack Obama small-donor fundraising effort that would seem to have been impossible in the absence of email, text messaging, online credit card donations, and social networking software. The data analysis presented in Chapters 4 and 5 will reveal more about changing contribution patterns in recent years, but for now, I turn to a review of the available data on how modern campaigns raise money.

Fundraising Patterns, 1980-2008

This variety of campaign, party, and group activity would have been difficult to analyze in the 1950s and 1960s. In reading the best scholarly works of the time, authored by Alexander Heard and Herbert Alexander, it is remarkable how much detail they were able to provide, considering the paucity of reliable information. The reporting requirements enacted in the 1970s now make it possible to analyze systematic data on campaign fundraising, and to examine important trends over time. In the remainder of this chapter, I provide an overview of the available data, focusing on the proportions of each type of funds raised by Senate, House, and presidential campaigns since the early 1980s.[13]

As Figure 3.1 shows, political fundraising has far outstripped the inflation rate, and has also grown in relation to the voting age population. As Ansolabehere, de Figuerido and Snyder point out, however, fundraising has remained relatively constant as a percent of Gross Domestic Product (Ansolabehere, de Figuerido, and Snyder 2003). This parallels developments in other similar areas of fundraising. As Figure 3.2 illustrates, charitable contributions – although much more widespread than political contributions – have also been relatively constant as a percentage of GDP.

Perhaps more interesting than the overall amount of fundraising is its distribution. As we saw in the introduction, according to self-reported survey data collected by the National Election Studies, the number of individual contributors has surged in recent years. Aside from a brief jump in the mid-1970s that can be attributed to a difference in survey question wording, the number of individual contributors today is higher than it has ever been. It is interesting to compare Figure 1.1 with Figure 3.2 – an increase in charitable giving roughly parallels the surge in individual contributing to political campaigns.

This rise in the number of individual contributions seems to be gradually reducing the extent to which campaigns rely on Political Action Committees (PACs). Figure 3.3 shows the percentage of funds collected from Political Action Committees by House and Senate campaigns in presidential election years from 1980 to 2008. House campaigns typically rely on PACs more than Senate campaigns, which have broader fundraising bases, but both types of campaigns have seen a gradual reduction in PAC fundraising and a corresponding increase in individual fundraising.

Figure 3.3: PAC Contributions as a Percent of All Receipts, House and Senate Campaigns, 1980-2008

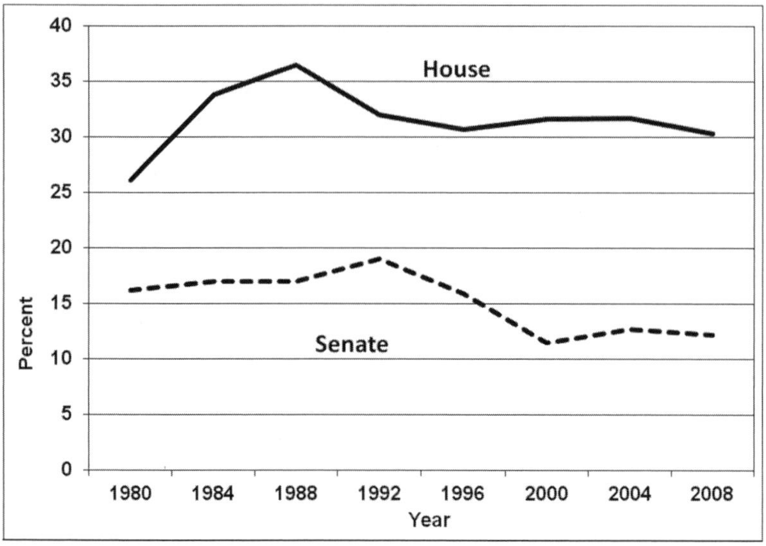

Source: Federal Election Commission.

Presidential campaigns, which rely almost entirely on individual contributions, have been broadening their fundraising bases in recent years. Partly this has occurred out of necessity: the rising cost of campaigns has caused an increasing number of candidates to opt out of the public financing system for presidential primary races, and after Barack Obama's success in 2008, future candidates are likely to decline the general election subsidy as well. This trend, combined with the elimination of "soft money" after the 2002 BCRA, has forced presidential campaigns to raise money from individuals in smaller amounts than in the past. It is possible that the rise in candidate-supporting "Super PACs" that emerged in the wake of the 2010 *Citizens United* v. *FEC* Supreme Court case could relieve some pressure on campaigns to expand their individual fundraising base, but it is too early to tell for sure whether this will be the case.

Individual contributions to presidential campaigns have increased, therefore, partly because of increased solicitation of individuals by presidential campaigns due to changes in the campaign environment. This seems unlikely to be the whole explanation for the more general increase in individual contributions, however, since it does not explain why congressional campaigns have also increased the proportion of their fundraising from individuals. One obvious additional factor is technological change. It is difficult to look at graphs such as Figures 1.1 and 3.2 and not think of the rise of the internet as a possible cause of the increase. Campaigns and contributors alike may be taking advantage of the ease with which transactions can take place online.

One simple way to test the plausibility of this argument is to observe whether campaigns have become more diverse in their fundraising in recent years. Innovation diffusion theory suggests that some actors will adopt a new technology earlier than others, depending in part on "the extent to which a technology offers improvements over currently available tools" (Dillon and Morris 1996, p. 10). In the case of political campaigns, certain campaigns should be expected to adopt new technologies faster or slower than others, and one might expect a greater focus on individual contributions among campaigns that have a comparative advantage in collecting them. (More on this point will come in later chapters.) Figure 3.4 provides a simple test of this possibility. I graph the standard deviation of the proportion of funds raised from individuals for House campaigns from 1984 to the present. For challengers and open-seat candidates – candidates that tend to rely disproportionately on individual contributions – the standard deviations have increased since 2000. For incumbents, who raise more money from PACs and rely less on individual contributions, the standard deviation has remained the same over time. These data are consistent with the theory that campaigns have adapted to a new technological environment at different rates. More broadly, the data are consistent with the theory that technological change has driven recent changes in individual contribution patterns.

Conclusion

Campaigns raise about the same amount of money as they ever have, relative to the size of the economy, but there have been several significant recent changes in how that money is raised. Individual contributions have become more important, and political action committee contributions less important, in congressional and presidential fundraising. In the context of U.S. history, however, the picture is more of consistency than of change. Since the demise of the assessment system at the end of the 19th century, parties and candidates alike have puzzled over how to solve collective action problems. They

Figure 3.4: Standard Deviation of Proportion of Funds Raised from Individuals, House Candidates, 1984-2010

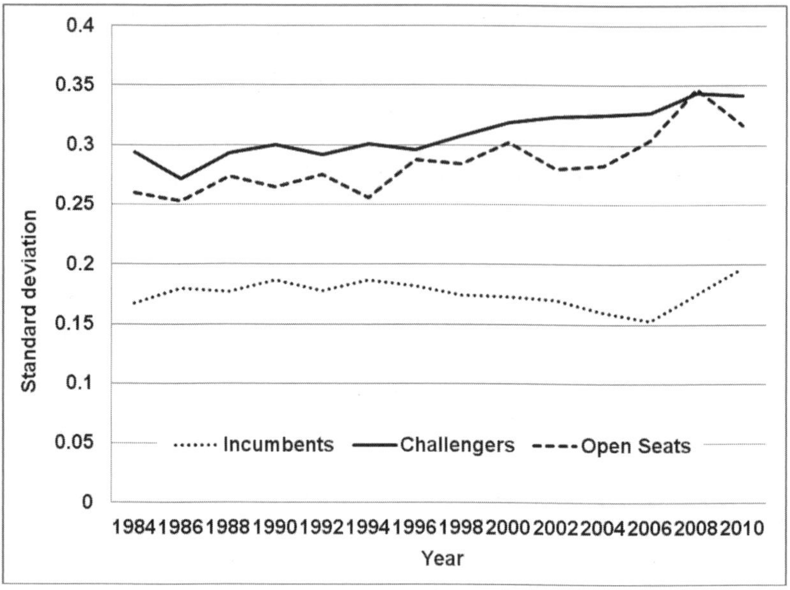

Source: Federal Election Commission Data

have relied on material, social, purposive, and expressive incentives in their efforts to do so.

Political parties and individual candidates have had the most consistent success in mobilizing via material and solidary incentives rather than through purposive and expressive incentives. Efforts such as the Jamieson plan that relied exclusively on purposive and expressive motives have fallen flat, except in rare cases in which extraordinary candidates piqued the interest of passionate segments of the public. Clark and Wilson, who argued in 1961 that purposive organizations were the least stable, would not be surprised by this historical fact. Small contributions from those with purposive or expressive motives do seem to go hand-in-hand with passion and enthusiasm, partly because passion overcomes the collective action problem, and partly because a contribution reinforces a person's commitment to a cause.

Today, most campaigns continue to rely on large contributions from individuals, and in some cases organizations, for the bulk of their funds.

Smaller contributions can play an important role, however, especially for candidates whose messages are outside the mainstream. As in the past, these small contributions can serve both as a source of money and as a tool with which campaigns and parties can stoke enthusiasm and effort on the part of their supporters.

The next three chapters focus on the role that individual contributors play in modern campaigns, and provide clearer and more specific tests of Chapter 2's potential explanations for why individuals contribute at all, and why they have contributed more in the last decade.

---

[1] The one percent figure comes from "Political Assessments," *New York Times*, April 3, 1880, p. 2; the two percent figure from "Political Assessments," *Washington Post*, July 14, 1879, p. 2. The two percent figure seems to be more commonly referenced.

[2] "Political Assessments," *New York Times*, April 3, 1880, p. 2.

[3] "Advertising that Pays," *Los Angeles Times*, January 27, 1892, p. 11.

[4] Herbert Welsh, "Campaign Committees: Publicity as a Cure for Corruption," *Forum*, September 1892, p. 26.

[5] Ibid., 26.

[6] "Democrats to Raise Big Fund," *Los Angeles Times*, August 25, 1919, p. 18.

[7] Glenn Thrush and Carrie Budoff Brown, "Obama's Deadline Dollar Dash," *Politico*, July 1, 2011, http://www.politico.com/news/stories/0611/58178.html, accessed July 1, 2011.

[8] "Abandon Idea of a Shakedown," *Los Angeles Times*, September 21, 1920, p. I15.

[9] Also see John J. Goldman, "McGovern Starts Push for Citizens' Donations," *Los Angeles Times*, August 20, 1972, p. 6.

[10] Research of Alexander Heard, cited in Sabato, p. 12.

[11] "Staff Bios," http://www.conservativehq.com/about, accessed June 23, 2011.

[12] Jonathan Martin and Maggie Haberman, "GOP Field Scrambles in Fall Cash Dash," *Politico*, September 26, 2011 http://www.politico.com/news/stories/0911/64387.html, accessed August 6, 2012.

[13] Data are available from the Federal Election Commission, www.fec.gov. I begin the analysis in 1982, since that is the earliest date for which the FEC reports summary data in electronic form.

4

How Modern Campaigns Appeal to Individual Contributors

Mark Neumann wasn't exactly an unknown in Wisconsin Republican circles. The onetime math teacher and businessman had represented the state's first congressional district in Congress from 1995 to 1999. He had run a respectable campaign against U.S. Senator Russ Feingold in 1998, coming within two percentage points of beating the popular incumbent. Still, by 2010, Neumann had been largely out of politics for over ten years. He was, therefore, very much an underdog in that year's race for the Republican nomination for governor.

Facing Neumann was Scott Walker, the Milwaukee County Executive who had run unsuccessfully for governor in 2006. Unbowed by that defeat, Walker had been running ever since, addressing Republican gatherings, laying out his plans, and formally announcing his candidacy in April 2009.

Neumann was a well-liked, engaging Wisconsin personality – he won a prize in a Milwaukee endurance contest to see who could hold a full beer stein, arm outstretched, the longest. But Neumann lacked the core of large-donor fundraisers that had mostly coalesced around Walker. A poll taken late in 2009 put Walker's support at more than double that of Neumann. Undeterred, Neumann decided to focus on grassroots networking. A staff of internet-savvy technology consultants with little experience in electoral politics rapidly mobilized a large base of supporters via online networking similar to MyBarackObama.com. The candidate began a Twitter account – one he used to "actually interact with his followers," as one liberal blogger put it, a bit impressed despite himself.[1] Neumann's Facebook friend list swelled. The campaign took on the giddy feeling of being on the forefront of something new. As a fundraiser who worked with the Neumann campaign describes it, our traditional fundraising platforms did not exist. Not because we didn't know how to implement them; we had no support. We were down 42 points. Your traditional donors, who most political candidates call to ask for a donation... are what I call "establishment donors" who were supporting the leading candidate. This was the first campaign I had ever experienced that we were able to change that model, and actually see it evolve in front of us.

When we started out, I think the campaign had a hundred online registered user accounts, and by the end of it, we had, on any given day, over 1,200 active user accounts. People [were] planning events every day, blogging every day, planning groups, sending out personal fundraising pages – and the way that we were able to grow our audience and support simply by using this platform was astonishing.[2]

Neumann's enthusiastic followers also contributed money. Wisconsin campaign finance records show that his average contribution in 2010 was $94, and the median contribution was $25.[3]

For Neumann supporters, this showed the promise of the new, more modern modes of campaigning. His chief fundraiser argued that the Neumann effort showed that the Barack Obama campaign of 2008 was not a unique event. "Barack Obama was an outstanding candidate, don't get me wrong. That's just the plain and simple truth. Mark Neumann, who I've always loved to death, and who I think would've been one of the best leaders our country has ever seen, was not as charismatic as Barack Obama, yet the platform worked as well as, and some would say even better than, it did for Barack Obama."[4] From this perspective, brand new forms of connecting with supporters and of soliciting their contributions appear set to transform modern campaign finance.

But in the end, Neumann lost his primary race to his more establishment-backed opponent, Scott Walker. To be sure, Neumann had advanced from being a long shot to garnering a respectable 38 percent of the primary vote. But should his campaign serve as an indicator of how campaigns have changed, or should it serve as a cautionary tale about the limits of new technology and new fundraising strategies? Was Neumann merely a modern William Jennings Bryan, Barry Goldwater, or George McGovern, with an enthusiastic following but no broad support?

Raising money in contemporary campaigns bears significant resemblance to past fundraising, but the introduction of new technologies prompts questions about how much the world has changed as a result. The example of Mark Neumann, to say nothing of the Obama and Ron Paul examples, suggest that individual contributions are easier to collect today than in previous eras, owing to new tools such as social networking, text messaging, and microtargeting (the ability of campaigns to precisely identify a voter's characteristics and to tailor appeals to him or her). These tools may have broadened the fundraising base – and may lead to further broadening in the future. From this perspective, the long-ago vision of the Jamieson plan may become the norm in U.S. politics.

But Neumann, Paul and Obama are exceptions to the rule – at least as campaigns stand today. Neumann did well in harnessing the new technology, but ultimately went down to defeat. Ron Paul, while more successful than in his 1988 race, still failed to attract widespread voter support in 2008 and 2012. And Barack Obama benefited in 2008 not only from his tech-savvy staff, but also from his unique life story and the grave economic crisis in which the nation found itself. Furthermore, later analysis revealed that Obama had received about the same percentage of his funds from small contributors as had previous campaigns – he just raised more from all sources than earlier candidates had.[5]

The most colorful and striking instances of fundraising, in other words, are those most likely to receive media attention, but the media often notice them precisely because they are unusual. Past candidates, too, from William Jennings Bryan to George McGovern, have generated excitement from small contributors – and did so in an era before the internet made credit card contributions so easy. The fundraising successes so prominent in press accounts are unrepresentative of the way most money is raised in modern campaigns. This may change in the future, but it has not changed yet.

This does not mean that small individual contributions are unimportant. To the contrary, as we have seen, their numbers are growing and they are clearly a key element of many campaigns. However, they make up only one piece of the fundraising puzzle. In building a fundraising coalition, candidates may devote extensive effort to raising money from small contributors, or they may choose instead to allocate minimal effort to those who donate smaller amounts, and instead devote their limited resources on raising other sources of funds, such as Political Action Committees (PACs), party committees, larger individual donors, and even the candidate's personal wealth.

In this chapter, I explore the contemporary fundraising scene, making an effort to get an accurate picture of how a variety of candidates raise money rather than focusing on just a few illustrative cases. I rely primarily on the accounts of professional fundraisers themselves, supplemented by published information about campaigns, candidates, and the modern political environment.

In gathering the information for this chapter, I spoke with fundraisers who have worked in campaigns at all levels, from state legislative races, to gubernatorial contests, to interest group financing, to races for Congress and the presidency. Some agreed to speak with me on the record; others spoke on the condition of anonymity. I make no claim that the people with whom I spoke represent a random sample, but I did succeed in speaking with roughly equal numbers of Democrats and Republicans. Most of the people I spoke with work for professional firms whose business is – at least in part – helping candidates to raise money. These professionals have many years – in some cases decades – of experience and are therefore in a good position to comment on how fundraising typically works, as well as on recent changes in the fundraising environment.

This chapter expands upon the data from the Federal Election Commission presented at the conclusion of the last chapter. That data is useful to view in light of the interviews because it provides a kind of 'validity check' on what fundraisers say they are doing. Sophisticated data analysis will appear in later chapters and will provide further evidence about how today's campaigns raise money. But the first-hand accounts provided in this chapter fill in parts of the overall picture that data cannot. In my interviews, I concentrated on questions related to how campaigns and consultants view the fundraising task – how they break down the business of raising money from the earliest days of the campaign, and how they view the tradeoffs between fundraising from one source over another.

I begin by examining congressional campaigns, and move on to discuss presidential campaigns, fundraising for groups that are unaffiliated with candidates, and the role of new technology in fundraising. To a surprising extent, modern fundraising resembles past fundraising. Experienced campaigners disagree about the potential for widespread change that may be offered by new technologies. Candidates evidently raise money from different sources in different ways, and do so for different reasons.

Congressional Campaign Fundraising

Today's average winning campaign for the U.S. House of Representatives costs approximately $1.4 million; the average winning campaign for Senate is close to $10 million, although this number varies due to differences between states.[6] Any candidate embarking on a race must therefore consider his or her sources of funding carefully, and must develop a plan for generating a cash pool in the neighborhood of this figure, with a consideration of how much one's opponent is expected to spend, how expensive the media market is, and other local factors. A typical modern congressional campaign raises funds from a variety of sources. Finance directors usually begin their calculations with what one fundraiser called "fundraising 101,"[7] mapping out potential sources of money in groups of people who have some personal relationship with a candidate. If a person is very close to a candidate socially, whether it be a college classmate, a family member, or a former co-worker, that person is a good prospect for a significant contribution.

Those with more distant connections, such as those who simply agree with the candidate's positions on issues (or disagree with his or her opponent), are less certain to pitch in. As one Democratic Party consultant explains it, in the beginning stages of the campaign "we sit down with the candidate, we brainstorm through their whole list – you know their rolodex list, their electronic list – anyone they've come in contact with in their life – and we quantify those individuals." [8] This quantification can be quite specific – involving specifying "ask" amounts for each person – and can therefore give the campaign a good sense of how much they are confident that they can raise. The process of estimating what each person is "worth" may seem crass, but this is the same kind of estimation process that takes place in fundraising in many other venues, such as college-level alumni fundraising drives or development campaigns undertaken by charitable organizations.

Another Democratic consultant agrees with this description of the process: "You start out with an individual's personal network and you branch out from there and take their entire personal history into account – all the way to where they went to elementary school, clubs, associations, accolades, so anything they've won as well, how long they've been involved politically, their profession and people that they've represented or clients that they've had in that profession, and keep going through there."[9]

This beginning phase of the fundraising process looks like what we could identify as an effort to mobilize James Q. Wilson's social ("solidary") incentives. As Wilson predicted, campaigns see personal connections as a powerful reason for contributing to a common cause. As the hypotheses discussed in Chapter 2 predict, a person's "embeddedness" in social networks does make it more likely that they will be solicited.

This social incentive is powerful enough that fundraisers do their best to get it to function even beyond a candidate's own circle of friends and family. In fact, some fundraisers view some kind of personal connection as being essential, even for contributors who have more remote connections with a candidate or cause. As one put it, "If they're a cold target – a cold prospect – and they've never given to a political campaign, it's very unlikely that you're going to receive a contribution unless there's some personal tie to that individual or some personal interest that you share with that individual."[10]

As a result of this need for a personal connection, a second step (after genuine personal contacts have been tapped) is to design a strategy that will allow candidates to establish a personal connection with those who may be strangers at the outset of a campaign. As one professional fundraiser puts it, "What we do [in our consulting practice] is we brainstorm with a candidate trying to come up with a personal story, a personal pitch, which first of all allows the candidate to create rapport over the phone with the donor. And from that personal pitch we get into issues and what's important to that specific donor."[11]

Because a feeling of connection will make it more likely for a person to contribute, candidates try to foster repeat connections with supporters as a means of ensuring an ongoing fundraising base. As one Democratic fundraiser puts it, "it's good to just see who your best friends have been over the last five, ten years, or however long the person has been in office."[12] In his detailed account of his political career, Representative David Price (D-NC) writes that in his first race for Congress "I cultivated potential donors carefully, calling on them personally and sending them a steady flow of information about the campaign" (Price 2004, p. 15). If a candidate is new to politics and therefore has few personal connections, he or she may seek out those who have been active in the party, or who have contributed regularly to similar candidates or causes. Richard Viguerie's use of Barry Goldwater's old campaign lists (see Chapter 3) is one example of this technique.

Another way that scholars and fundraisers alike think about sources of funds is in terms of the three or four types of contributor that correspond with categories visible in Federal Election Commission filings, including Political Action Committees (PACs), large individual contributors, and small individual contributors. Several fundraisers confirmed that these are not just artificial categories created by the FEC – fundraisers do often think in general terms about how much money is available from each source.

PACs make up about one-third of the typical House candidate's contributions and a smaller proportion of typical Senate candidates' contributions. These organizations are sometimes easily identifiable as ideologically-motivated, but most are associated with firms that have no obvious ideological agenda. Some reformers argue that corporate PACs necessarily have a "pro-business" agenda, but there are actually very few political organizations that see their mandate as protecting the interests of business as a whole (Smith 2000). More often, PACs focus on the narrow interests of their own firms, which may concern conventionally conservative and free market goals, but may also lead some to promote increased government regulation or intervention in the economy if such actions benefit a firm (or harm the firm's competitors) (Mitchell & Munger 1991; McChesney 1997).

In the late 1990s, sociologists Clawson, Neustadtl, & Weller did an admirable job of canvassing PAC directors for their views on when and why they contributed. Their interviews revealed that PACs give for a number of different reasons, from the hope for simple material benefits, to more complex combinations of social and ideological considerations. What is more, PACs can be less certain of their choices and more internally divided than other kinds of donors, due to the diverse membership on PAC boards, the relationships between PACs and their parent organizations (which can have diverse interests), and debates over whether to (for example) give to incumbents who will be more likely to hold power or to challengers who are more likely to mirror the ideological views of the PAC itself. Serious conflict on PAC boards is rare, but it can occur, at times because incentives for giving may be at odds with one another. A PAC official interviewed by Clawson and his colleagues described one such instance:

> From my perspective, it is somewhat of an embarrassment with our PAC, but it's only one candidate. We contribute to him every year and he doesn't have a pro-business voting record. He just happens to be a *frat brother* of the number three person in the company (Clawson, Neustadtl, & Weller 1998, p. 46, emphasis in original).

It is telling that even in the case of a PAC, in this instance a social consideration overrode an ideological one.

The complexity of PAC contribution decisions notwithstanding, scholars have tended to divide PACs into two general groups. Non-ideological (or "pragmatic") PACs contribute mostly to incumbents, calculating that it is better to have access to a member of Congress who will likely be around for a while than to take chances in supporting a challenger. Most ideological PACs (a small minority) adopt a different strategy, spending their money in ways that will affect the outcome of elections. As a result, these PACs divide their spending about equally between incumbents and challengers. (One easy way to calculate a back-of-the-envelope figure for ideological PACs is to focus on "non-connected" PACs – PACs that have no parent corporate or union sponsor. Treating all 'connected' PACs as pragmatic is probably incorrect, however, since some PACs with corporate and union connections are clearly ideological in their giving patterns.)

A campaign cannot know for sure exactly how its fundraising efforts will turn out, but savvy finance directors and consultants can estimate in advance which PAC contributions are available to it, and how much certain PACs are willing to give:

> Some candidates are pro choice, and even in Democratic primaries some candidates are pro-life. If you're pro-life that's a specific targeted amount of money from Democratic interest groups because some of these PACs – say like NARAL and Planned Parenthood – are not going to contribute to someone who's anti-choice. If you're not pro labor the labor unions are not going to contribute to you. So we're able to break down all the PACs in DC according to industry and determine how much we can get from each industry. That's your PAC potential.[13]

Because there are far fewer ideological PACs than pragmatic PACs, the vast majority of PAC money goes to those who already hold office. In 2010, according to data compiled by the Center for Responsive Politics, 79 percent of PAC money went to incumbents.[14] A challenger may therefore find that this source of funding is simply not available. The lack of PAC funding would prompt such a challenger to devote most of his or her efforts to one or more of the other available sources of funds.

A second category that is useful to consider separately is "large" contributions from individuals. What constitutes a "large" contribution is in one sense a subjective matter – for some people a $100 gift seems large, but for others $5,000 is a pittance. One useful way to place a boundary on the "large" category, however, is to base it on existing regulatory designations. The FEC requires that candidates itemize a contribution if it is $200 or above. Contributions below that level, therefore, are considered (at least by the regulators) to be so small as to not require detailed accounting.

The upper bound of "large" contributions is also easily specified by the law. Current limits (as of 2012) allow contributors to give up to $2,500 to a candidate for each election he or she contests, meaning that a contributor may give up to $5,000 for each election cycle, since each cycle includes both a primary election and a general election.

Considered as any contribution from $200 to the $5,000 maximum, "large" contributions make up 38 percent of the average amount raised by candidates for the House of Representatives and 40 percent of the average amount raised by Senate candidates. House incumbents raise 41 percent of their funds from large contributors, while challengers raise 36 percent from this source.[15]

Candidates, scholars, and courts alike have found it useful to consider relatively large contributions separately from the smaller ones, and have often justified these distinctions based on presumed differences in the motivation for giving them. In examining campaign contribution limits for the first time, the Supreme Court speculated that contributions were less expressive than other forms of political activity, but that varying contribution amounts might serve as an indicator of the donor's intensity of support:

> A contribution serves as a general expression of support for the candidate and his views, but does not communicate the underlying basis for the support. The quantity of communication by the contributor does not increase perceptibly with the size of his contribution, since the expression rests solely on the undifferentiated, symbolic act of contributing. At most, the size of the contribution provides a very rough index of the intensity of the contributor's support for the candidate.[16]

On the one hand, the Court seems skeptical that contributions are an effective means of political communication, and seems to question why contributors give at all. On the other, the Court provides one hypothesis about how larger contributors may differ from smaller contributors: in the intensity of their support for a candidate. From this perspective, larger contributors are those who feel most passionately about the election of a particular candidate to office. This may encompass those who are closest to the candidate personally, such as relatives, friends, past roommates, and so on. It is also possible that those who are ideologically more committed to a candidate's policy positions might disproportionately fill this group, as the Supreme Court implies.

But the opposite state of affairs is also plausible – that the largest contributors are in fact the least likely to be ideologically-driven. From this perspective, large contributors are more interested in material benefits for themselves and their affiliates, and view these material incentives as being more available to large contributors than to smaller ones. Historically, party and candidate fundraisers have found that larger contributions are more readily available if material and solidary incentives are at work (see Chapter 3). Chief among the material incentives that candidates can offer is access – a commodity that is especially valuable if the candidate is an incumbent elected official.

This view of large contributions as investments (or even as "purchases" of a certain amount of access), corresponds with what at least one fundraiser characterized as the reluctance of large donors to contribute unless they see the campaign as being effective enough to hold out the possibility of the candidate winning – and therefore of their investment paying off. As this Democratic fundraiser put it, "A lot of times you may need to wait on the major donors in the area because they want to see that they're not the only ones investing into the race. You want to prove your viability. It doesn't mean that you don't speak to them, but you've got to really cultivate a relationship and demonstrate that you're actually running a legit campaign before they can actually move forward with a donation."[17] This explanation is consistent with Mark Neumann's inability to attract large contributions in his campaign for governor of Wisconsin.

Whether larger contributors are more ideologically committed than smaller contributors, or whether they are less so, is a matter I will return to in the next chapter. For now, it is enough to point out that the experiences of fundraisers suggest that there is good reason to treat this category of contributions as theoretically distinct from smaller ones.

Finally, candidates may raise funds from small individual contributions. Again, although what constitutes "small" may be subjective, amounts less than $200 are lumped together by most campaigns for the purposes of FEC reporting, so it is convenient to think of small contributions as those of $200 or less. This classification scheme places the 2008 Obama campaign's estimate of its average contribution (about $90) squarely within the "small" category.

Placing small contributions in a separate category allows us to consider the possibility that the motives of the small contributor differ substantially from those of larger contributors. When Barack Obama and his staff justified their decision to opt out of the general election public financing system in 2008, they made such an argument. Small contributions, Obama argued, are less likely to be corrupting because they are less likely to be motivated by hope of personal (material) gain.

According to the Supreme Court's reasoning (above), smaller contributors are likely to be those who feel the least intensely about the election of the candidate. They may be more or less indifferent, and contribute because the cost of doing so is relatively low. Political scientists have sometimes used similar reasoning to explain why people pay the "cost" of voting. When the amounts involved are trivial, a strict cost-benefit calculus may be less useful (Aldrich 1993).

An alternative theory would suggest that those who give the least are the most ideologically committed. If larger contributors expect material rewards for their substantial contributions, smaller contributors have less reason to expect to be rewarded for pitching in $10 (or even $110) to a political campaign. Under those circumstances, smaller donors would be mostly devoid of material concerns, and more focused on other types of incentives. These might include intense ideological commitment. Indeed, the historical examples of William Jennings Bryan, Barry Goldwater, and George McGovern – to say nothing of Ron Paul and Barack Obama – suggest that this might be the case.

Interviews with fundraisers go some distance towards resolving the question of which of these two theories is correct.

Fundraisers report that raising money in small amounts – even in the age of internet donations – is difficult and time consuming, especially if a candidate is not already a well known figure. As a Democratic consultant put it, internet fundraising is "not very easy. It's easier to raise [money that way] when you're running for President of the United States....If you're a first-time person running for the U.S. Congress or even if you are a United States Congressperson, it's tough to engage an internet fundraising system in your campaign."[18]

Even in the area of this small-donor fundraising, campaigns seek to mobilize personal networks of connections – just as they do with large "bundlers." As one Democratic fundraiser put it, "There's only so much time and you can't necessarily build a relationship with every single major donor. What you can do is build a great relationship with one person who is well connected or who has a completely different network that you wouldn't normally be able to access."[19]

Personal networks are one tool that campaigns can use to mobilize small contributors, but they do not shy away from all sorts of techniques – whether they are social, material, or cause-oriented. As one Democratic fundraiser put it, "A lot of small donor fundraising is based on gimmicks – either it's a challenge that you match someone else's fundraising, or it's 'so and so said this, help me respond by giving $25 or whatever it may be, or contribute now and you get a mug or you get entered into a contest." This same fundraiser hastens to add that the ideological concerns of the contributor are an underlying factor in his or her decision to donate, whether or not such "gimmicks" are effective. "My former boss used to say that a vacuum cleaner salesman doesn't sell vacuums, he sells clean floors. So you're selling the end result or the cause and not necessarily the specific tool you used to bring something in, whether it's a contest or an event or something."[20]

In sum, although some fundraising tactics work more effectively than others in some situations, campaigns seem to employ a variety of social, material, and ideological incentives for raising money, especially when it comes to small contributors. Combinations of these techniques may be more effective than any single technique used on its own, or it may be the case that it is difficult for campaigns to tell exactly what will motivate a particular contributor. Small contributors do seem to have consistent purposive or expressive motives, but may also need to be prodded with social or material inducements.

Contemporary Presidential Campaign Fundraising

Federal Election Commission reports on presidential fundraising look similar to reports on House and Senate fundraising, with a few significant exceptions. The total amounts raised are larger – especially for the candidates who win major party nominations, but the real difference between presidential sources of funds and Congressional sources of funds is that presidential candidates collect very few – if any – contributions from Political Action Committees. There are several reasons for this. The most practical is that there is a finite number of PACs (around 4,000). Even if each PAC contributed the maximum $10,000 to a presidential candidate, the total (about $40 million) would fall far short of the amount necessary to run an effective presidential campaign – even in the primaries.[21] Just as Senate candidates rely less on PACs than do House candidates, presidential candidates rely less on PACs than Senate candidates do. This fact sheds a new light on the frequent pledges of presidential candidates that they will refuse PAC funds on principle: In fact, they would not have raised much money from PACs anyway.

Presidential candidates focus instead on building coalitions of wealthy people to solicit other wealthy people, just as political parties did a century ago. Since at least the Clinton administration, campaigns have aggressively cultivated those who are effective "bundlers," establishing particular "levels" for those who raise benchmark amounts of $100,000 or more. George W. Bush called his $100,000 bundlers "Pioneers," and later added two new levels – "Rangers" (for those raising at least $200,000) and "Super Rangers" (at least $300,000) for the 2004 campaign. Bush appointed 188 of their number to administration positions, according to the watchdog group Public Citizen.[22] Despite his reputation for small dollar fundraising, Barack Obama followed the Bush model, raising about the same proportion of his funds from these sources as did previous campaigns. The Center for

Public Integrity found that 184 of Obama's top fundraisers were appointed to some role in the administration.[23]

Presidential fundraising differs from other fundraising because of the sheer organizational infrastructure that is involved. As one Republican fundraising consultant put it,

> Presidential Campaigns are different [from other campaigns] because they are really large conglomerate organizations. Very rarely does the candidate [interact personally with contributors]. As a matter of fact, in 2008 I did an event with President Bush who was coming to North Carolina for a fundraising event for the candidate I was working for. And what is different is there is not any candidate interaction. It's all organization based.[24]

In one intriguing study of very large contributors (McCarty, Poole and Rosenthal 2006), the authors find that the largest contributors behave as if they are giving for ideological reasons rather than for material ones. In the study, the authors find that the largest individual contributions of soft money to political parties (an unregulated form of giving that was legal prior to 2002) came from donors who are at the ideological fringes. They conclude that "even if the parties do not use these soft money contributions exclusively for the benefit of their extreme members, such large sums from ideological contributors must make the parties more responsive to the extreme ideological views" (McCarty, Poole & Rosenthal 2006, p. 158). (Because large "soft money" contributions to political parties such as the ones studied here are no longer allowed under the law, such contributors today must go elsewhere to influence the political process – perhaps to super PACs or other independent groups.)

The tendency of big contributors to be more ideological appears to support the Supreme Court's hypothesis in *Buckley* that larger contributions are a rough indicator of intensity of support. On the other hand, as discussed above, an equally plausible hypothesis suggests that larger contributions might be less ideologically motivated than others. The liberal groups that have targeted conservative entrepreneurs Charles and David Koch have often argued that their largesse is due to their pursuit of lenient treatment for their business concerns – a material rather than ideological motive.

This suggests a situation in which there may be rapid diminishing returns to material benefits that result from contributions. One dollar is unlikely to generate a material benefit to the contributor. One thousand dollars might generate some sort of material favor. One hundred thousand, however, might not purchase much more.

In securing these large contributors, presidential campaigns try their utmost to trade in the currency of prestige. At fundraising dinners, for example, more generous donors get seated nearer to the candidate. In the Clinton era, the White House embroiled itself in controversy when journalists discovered that major donors received invitations to spend a night (or several) in the White House's Lincoln Bedroom.

Finally, presidential campaigns can sometimes generate waves of small contributions, as the example of the 2008 Obama campaign illustrates. Obama achieved tremendous success in collecting cash from a vast pool of small donors, but Ron Paul's campaigns were in many ways more driven by small contributors than were Obama's. As the account at the beginning of Chapter 1 shows, his supporters aggressively promoted fundraising via staged events such as the Guy Fawkes day "money bomb." Other presidential efforts such as that of Michele Bachmann in 2012, have also seen success with targeting small donors across the country. A common characteristic of these campaigns is that they have clear, distinct, principle-driven messages – characteristics that make them more attractive to purposive and expressive contributors than other campaigns (see Chapter 2).

Contemporary Party and Group Fundraising

Parties and groups are allowed to collect money from individuals in larger amounts than are candidates, so large individual contributions make up the bulk of party and group givers. For groups that are affiliated with companies or unions, their natural support base is clear. Groups that are non-connected usually have a particular issue concern and focus on raising money from those who are sympathetic to these concerns. As Theda Skocpol and Steven Schier, among others, have pointed out, these groups find long-distance fundraising via direct mail or other techniques to be more efficient than through decentralized local organizational structures (Skocpol 2003; Schier 2000).

Interest groups (as opposed to political parties) benefit from relaxed fundraising rules that allow them to seek the support of large benefactors. Nearly two decades ago, political scientist David Walker recognized the importance of these "philanthropic" foundations and individuals in giving life and sustenance to many key groups in Washington. More recently, sponsors such as David and Charles Koch on the right and George Soros on the left have each sponsored interest groups that have participated vigorously in key political campaigns.

Some credit the Kochs with giving rise to the entire Tea Party movement, but it is more likely that for them, as in the case of the Obama campaign, grassroots enthusiasm was a crucial component of their efforts.

Those who have raised money for interest groups confirm that larger contributors are more important for these groups than for the typical candidate: "I think the approach for a 527 is a lot of times we put a lot of time and effort into a handful of leads. A lot of those organizations are funded by 20 or 30 donors who are each doing $50,000, $100,000, sometimes $500,000 checks, so a lot of it is strategy and planning and building relationships with donors in various networks."[25]

The Role of New Technology

New technology has at a minimum changed some features of the process of fundraising. Whereas direct mail and the telephone were once the only tools in the fundraiser's arsenal, today there are many more tools that allow campaigns to reach out to potential contributors in new ways. These technologies range from the simple to the complex, and are used in varying ways by the campaigns that take advantage of them.

Email

One of the oldest of the "new" technologies, email represents a natural way to reach voters and potential contributors alike. According to the Pew Research Center, 92 percent of Americans use email – a figure that makes the medium an especially tempting one for reaching people.[26]

Email has indeed become a major source for campaign fundraising – especially for those who do not give the largest amounts of money. One Republican fundraiser at a firm that specializes in online fundraising says the job

> pretty much centers around drafting and sending out a lot of emails and also building massive email lists. I would say probably right now 80 to 90 percent of the money that's raised online, certainly on the Republican side – and I've talked to competitors to our company who work on the other side who confirm this – it's all raised through email these days. People aren't going to websites as much anymore. We have to go out and find them and push them to a donations page, so it's more of a direct push through the combination of emails and online ads we're able to find people who will somehow connect with our candidate or organization's message.[27]

As this fundraiser suggests, fundraising by email is not as simple as it might seem, however. It would be a mistake to think of it as costless, for example. Another fundraiser explained why:

> Email is not free. When you're building a list you have to find individuals' emails like any corporation does. So I mean it just doesn't make sense to have a list of 100,000 people or 200,000 people and have an intern sitting there trying to find emails for each individual – it's too time-consuming. What we're able to do [at our firm] is we're able to find people's emails within a couple of hours. So email is free, sending email is free, but researching and accessing individual donors' email addresses is not free.[28]

This fundraiser emphasizes the importance of a good, well-targeted list: "Just sending out an email that says 'contribute to me, I'm running for Congress, and this is why,' it's very ineffective."[29] Another fundraiser agrees: "I just think that it's a misconception of politics to think it's just about sending an email and if people don't know [the candidate] they'd be willing to give."[30]

This means that consultants and candidates must get creative in securing lists of email addresses:

> We're able [at our firm] to build lists through friendly organizations, emailing their supporters on behalf of a candidate. Online ads are also a big source of gathering emails. People go to the website and sign up. It's sort of a variety of different ways that a campaign can acquire email addresses.[31]

Email therefore serves as an important tool for modern fundraising, but not a tool that has transformed the way fundraising works in a fundamental way. Candidates and fundraising professionals still must research prospects and appeal to them via calculated, often costly and time consuming, methods.

Websites

One way that candidates can gather email addresses is to draw visitors to the campaign's official websites. As several fundraisers interviewed point out, online advertisements can draw visitors to these websites, as can controversial or noteworthy events reported in the media. One fundraiser for a congressional campaign explains that drawing emails from website visitors is much more efficient than alternative methods. "Folks can also go to the website to sign up for emails – people do buy email lists, but I don't think that is all that effective to be totally honest, because you'll get folks to unsubscribe. You want people who want to be on [your list], because then you'll get the most out of it. And so that's how you really grow it, is directing people from our website and asking for email addresses."[32]

Campaigns view their websites as a means of disseminating information to interested voters and as sources of contact information for people who are interested in the campaign. Not insignificantly, modern websites also include ways for individuals to speedily make contributions via credit card. Finance directors see these sites as complementary to other methods of fundraising.

Social Networking Sites

Technology buffs and political consultants alike have touted the importance of social networking to modern political campaigns. In an early instance of a campaign taking online networking seriously, the John Edwards campaign became the first establish a campaign headquarters on the "virtual reality" site Second Life in 2007, in hopes that it would become a place for supporters to congregate and mobilize. As the virtual HQ's developer told the technology publication ZDNet, "with the campaign season starting so early, it's more important to win volunteers and supporters than votes at this point. An SL presence encourages that as well as any other initiative I can think of."[33]

Edwards's Second Life venture had a bumpy road – it was trashed by online vandals just weeks after it launched – but other campaigns have explored more popular forums like Facebook and Twitter ever since. Some have achieved tremendous success in mobilizing their supporters via these networks – most famously when the Barack Obama campaign created the Facebook clone "MyBarackObama.com" site. But Obama is not the only candidate to have benefited. Other candidates have worked to build similar networks – both on Facebook and on proprietary social networking sites.

One of the great advantages of Facebook for businesses has been its ability to precisely target advertising towards the particular group a business is interested in reaching. But this feature seems to have fallen short in terms of its fundraising potential. The Republican online fundraising expert quoted above confirms this generalization: "Facebook has not proved to be a really great source of fundraising, and that's also been confirmed by our competitors. It'll generate a lot of activity and action but that action doesn't necessarily translate into a lot of money."[34]

Microtargeting

Like email, microtargeting can be thought of as an extension of a previously existing campaign technique – that of tailoring the message to one's audience of the moment. For as long as politicians have run for office, they have been careful to adjust their speeches to, say, address labor issues before the AFL-CIO, business issues before the Chamber of Commerce, and education issues before the PTO. Modern microtargeting allows campaigns to hone this practice to a science, using dozens of variables to predict which issues are most likely to interest, say, an email recipient, and adjusting the content of that email accordingly.

Change vs. More of the Same

The fundraisers with whom I spoke disagree about how much new technology has changed fundraising. Some pointed out that the bulk of campaign money still comes from old-fashioned "candidate on the telephone" solicitation. "I would say for most it's going to be the candidate on the phone," says one Democratic fundraiser. "And that's going to be [true for] everything through members of Congress and candidates for U.S. Senate....Internet fundraising is probably – and again, dependent on the candidate – not as large a percentage as you might be led to believe by people talking about how great internet fundraising is."[35]

One fundraiser stresses that even if technology appears to be behind the fundraising surge in recent campaigns, more traditional networks of interpersonal connections have been at play as well, and are just as – if not more – important: The 2008 fundraising total

> comes from a great organizing effort, but at the same time there were a ton of people forwarding emails to friends with their personal endorsement of Barack or Hillary and the friend was like 'oh, if he's on board, maybe I should donate $25 bucks so he can stop bothering me,' or because they like the candidate. ...If you got a random email from a political candidate, would you contribute just because you got that email or does there have to be something more there? I think there's got to be something more there for someone to contribute.[36]

Many of the fundraisers with whom I talked expressed a similar discomfort with attributing a vast change to new technology, even as they acknowledged that email, microtargeting, and other technological innovation had altered the strategic calculus in some sense. Most argued that some other, more traditional, impetus to contributing has to be present as well, even if a potential contributor is reached in a new and different way.

Other professionals are more sanguine about the potential for new technology to bring fundamental changes to fundraising. They argue, first, that even if one concedes that the basic strategies of fundraising have remained stable, there are clear efficiency gains from new technology:

> with the new tools it's really sped up the process. Back in the nineties, you didn't have the access to individuals' information that you do now, and how it worked was, you went down to the state board of elections and pulled the actual paper copies of candidates' campaign filing reports and you literally had volunteers sit there and look up numbers in telephone books. Then it changed – you got telephone directories on CDs, and that helped quite a bit. Now, all we have to do is electronically develop a list, and then use modern marketing techniques and ascertain telephone numbers and emails.[37]

As an example of how microtargeting technology has made the process more efficient, one Republican fundraising consultant describes how his firm analyzes data on potential contributors:

> I analyze 647 variables of fundraising operations that I've learned or I've tested that have some sort of impact on the overall success of that fundraising operation. These variables can be anything and everything. They're not some secret. It could be how people give, where people give, the timing, you know, the frequency. All of those things, we throw into a model that we calculate and we come up with our own way of measuring what the likelihood is that that person will give again to the same candidate or even to a new candidate.[38]

Even those who stress traditional fundraising techniques such as the role of personal candidate solicitation acknowledge that new technology has made old practices more efficient. As one Democratic fundraiser put it,

> in that sense it's very important. And you know, there's certainly something to be said for [the argument that] if the candidate makes a call, and you have good data, and you enter it correctly, and you call that person three months later, and on the sheet in front of the candidate it says this is what you talked about last time, this is what the person's response was, this is the things we know about them – that's a big deal. And in the past, that wasn't something that you were able to do. Or if you were able to do it, you wrote it by hand on a

piece of paper, and that piece of paper was the exact same piece of paper they saw before. Now, that's not really the way that works anymore. Now, we can enter data, we can search by it, we can do whatever we want with it, and if we ever have to look at that person's record again, we know what their situation is, we know what we can be asking for or what their response was last time. We can be more informed as we talk to them.[39]

Others are even more enthusiastic about the transformative power of new technology, arguing that in addition to efficiency gains, new technologies can open up entirely new strategies for candidates. Such strategies may be especially important to candidates who faced limited fundraising options in the past. As one put it, these technologies

> may not have changed the fact that people still vote for candidates they like, but what they have done is change the way that candidates can communicate with voters. Particularly for insurgent candidates and opposition candidates, the internet is and I think will be the leading way for people to voice their opposition, and to support their candidate financially. We have had candidates raise a hundred thousand dollars in one day, online, so for a finance director to say that the internet hasn't changed the way that campaigns are run – it's astonishing to hear that. We've raised seven figures for a number of different candidates. I think when you put a million dollars in the bank for a candidate, that fundamentally changes the way a campaign is run.[40]

A Republican fundraiser suggests that some of the disagreement about the impact of new technology concerns the fact that campaigns have not yet determined how best to maximize the potential uses of these techniques. Those who are skeptical of its impact may not have seen its full potential. By building on past principles of campaigning, such as social ties, this fundraiser argues, campaigns can greatly increase their donor base:

> the truth of the matter is, the [impact of new technology] is unknown. … What I think technology has done is allow an entirely new philosophy that Barack Obama championed and that I am absolutely fascinated by. The whole campaign structure that he created was based on the notion that political campaigns have traditionally done one-way marketing or push marketing. But he understood that instead of trying to reach the masses of people by communicating Barack's platform positions to everyone just because of their likelihood of being a Democrat or an unaffiliated voter, if they could – if I already supported the campaign, then they could give me the tools and resources I needed, and the ability to communicate through a personal

way with you as a friend of mine, it would be much likelier that you would end up supporting the campaign because of your relationship with me, not your relationship with the campaign.[41]

The effectiveness of personal relationships is an element of campaigning and fundraising that has been known to campaign professionals for decades, but new social networking technology may allow these personal relationships to be used in large-scale campaign techniques, in addition to the small-scale, face-to-face techniques that in the past have generated funds from more insular groups of large contributors.

As this discussion suggests, part of the disagreement about the revolutionary nature of online fundraising may have to do with variation in the degree to which candidates rely on small contributors, and on the technologies that make it easier to reach them. Some candidates focus more on raising small individual contributions than others, and are more effective at doing so. The fundraiser who stressed the importance of the new technology for insurgents and underdogs is making a version of this point.

Insurgents and underdogs who have sharp, clear, and polarizing messages are more likely to appeal to those small contributors motivated by purposive incentives. New technologies can be helpful to such candidates by helping to transmit those messages to those who are more likely to be mobilized by them. As another Republican fundraiser who works for a firm that specializes in online fundraising says,

> This goes for the right and the left – any candidate who is willing to be more free in terms of going on TV and saying what some people might think are outrageous comments that not only motivate the people who agree with them because they're out there saying what these people think, but also motivates their political opponents because it enrages the other side and gets their supporters fired up and rallying around them. Typically, people are not going to raise that much money if they're in the middle. You've got to be on one side or another. And this is the same in all direct marketing with mail, phones, internet – it's difficult to raise money for people who are being very diplomatic in their public statements.[42]

Just as Clark and Wilson predict (see Chapter 2), those seeking to solve the collective action via purposive incentives appeal to ideological goals. It is interesting to point out one way in which the above statement defies Clark and Wilson's prediction, however. They state that although ideological statements are important, purposive organizations feel the need to be vague in their goals for fear of alienating current or potential members. This does not seem accurate if we accept the claim that candidates find it useful to make "outrageous comments" that are presumably specific and extremist. The data analysis in the chapters to follow will address this point further. But one explanation for this contradiction between Clark and Wilson's observations and those of today's fundraisers may be that the much larger audiences that are accessible to modern campaigns allow for narrower messages that motivate a small percentage of people. If the audience is big enough, even a tiny percentage can generate contributions that are sufficient to sustain a reasonable campaign. In using technology to target very specific audiences, modern campaigns may find clarity and specificity to be quite useful.

Candidates who find it prohibitively difficult to raise cash in one segment of the "market," therefore, may find that new technologies and new techniques open doors to them that might not have existed previously. Mark Neumann might have been unable to run an effective campaign had he been a candidate in the 1980s, but he was able to become formidable by focusing his efforts in the new area of social networking and small contributions. Just as Ron Paul had more success in 2008 than in 1988, new tools may given candidates some added flexibility that they might not have had before.

One point that most of the fundraisers I talked with agreed on is that new technology in the fundraising environment, like other new technologies introduced into various industries, has increased the overall productivity of fundraising efforts. This increase in productivity may be more obvious in some areas than in others, but there are ways in which technology has aided the productivity of even the oldest and most traditional fundraising methods, such as on-the-phone solicitation by the candidate.

Another way in which technology has assisted fundraising efforts has been to reduce the transaction costs involved in making a contribution. As the economist Douglass North defines transaction costs, they are "the costs of measuring the valuable attributes of what is being exchanged and the costs of protecting rights and policing and enforcing agreements" (North 1990, p. 27). It may seem odd to think of a campaign contribution as a two-way exchange, but as the discussion in Chapter 2 suggests, contributors receive some sort of "benefit" (material, solidary, purposive, or expressive). The costs of protecting rights and enforcing agreements can be viewed as referring to any number of costs that may be incurred in a transaction, from paying a real estate agent to assist in buying and selling a home, to the fees a credit card company may assess on retail transactions.

In any case, campaigns do their best to subsidize transaction costs that voters face – everything from bringing voter registration cards to people's doorsteps to shuttling people to the polls in campaign vans is designed to do this. But there are some transaction costs that, try as they might, campaigns cannot directly pay, such as the cost in time and effort of writing a check, inserting it into an envelope, and sticking it in a mailbox. New technology allows contributors to simply click on a button on a website, making the entire transaction much quicker and easier than it was in the past. These lower transaction costs make solving the collective action problem a simpler task for fundraisers than it was in the past, although they are still faced with the problem of how to make the cost of a contribution itself worthwhile.

---

[1] Cory Liebmann, "Walker v. Neumann: The Twit-Off," http://eye-on-wisconsin.blogspot.com/2009/07/walker-v-neumann-twit-off.html.

[2] Interview with Neal Harrington, President, Harrington Forward Thinking, August 8, 2011.

[3] Calculated by author from data available on the Wisconsin Campaign Finance Information System, http://cfis.wi.gov/; Neumann's contributions to his own campaign are excluded from this calculation.

[4] Interview with Neal Harrington, President, Harrington Forward Thinking, August 8, 2011.

[5] Campaign Finance Institute, "Reality Check: Obama Received About the Same Percentage from Small Donors in 2008 as Bush in 2004," November 24, 2008, http://www.cfinst.org/Press/PReleases/08-11-24/Realty_Check_-_Obama_Small_Donors.aspx, accessed July 23, 2012.

[6] OpenSecrets.org, http://www.opensecrets.org/bigpicture/elec_stats.php?cycle=2010, accessed August 22, 2011.

[7] Interview with Democratic Party fundraiser with experience in congressional campaigns, June 16, 2011.

[8] Interview with Doug Jaraczewski, President and Founder, Campaign Finance Group, June 30, 2011.

[9] Interview with Scott Dworkin, Founder and CEO, Bulldog Finance Group, July 5, 2011.

[10] Interview with Doug Jaraczewski, President and Founder, Campaign Finance Group, June 30, 2011.

[11] Interview with Doug Jaraczewski, President and Founder, Campaign Finance Group, June 30, 2011.

[12] Interview with Democratic Party fundraiser with experience in congressional campaigns, June 16, 2011.

[13] Interview with Doug Jaraczewski, President and Founder, Campaign Finance Group, June 30, 2011.

[14] Center for Responsive Politics, "PAC Dollars to Incumbents, Challengers, and Open Seat Candidates," http://www.opensecrets.org/bigpicture/pac2cands.php?cycle=2010, accessed July 20, 2012.

[15] Calculated by author from 2006 FEC summary files.

[16] *Buckley* v. *Valeo* 424 U.S. 1 (1976), p. 21.

[17] Interview with Scott Dworkin, Founder and CEO, Bulldog Finance Group, July 5, 2011.

[18] Interview with Doug Jaraczewski, President and Founder, Campaign Finance Group, June 30, 2011.

[19] Interview with Democratic Party fundraiser with experience in federal campaigns, July 21, 2011.

[20] Interview with Democratic Party fundraiser with experience in federal campaigns, July 21, 2011.

[21] $40 million was only about five percent of the total raised by the 2008 Obama campaign.

[22] "Rangers and Pioneers Receiving Appointments from the Bush Administration," Public Citizen and Texans for Public Justice, August 10, 2004, http://www.whitehouseforsale.org/documents/appoint0804.pdf, accessed December 14, 2011.

[23] Fred Schulte, John Aloysius Farrell and Jeremy Bordon, "Obama Rewards Big Bundlers with Jobs, Commissions, Stimulus Money, Government Contracts, and More," Center for Public Integrity, June 15, 2011, http://www.iwatchnews.org/2011/06/15/4880/obama-rewards-big-bundlers-jobs-commissions-stimulus-money-government-contracts-and, accessed December 14, 2011.

[24] Interview with Neal Harrington, President, Harrington Forward Thinking, August 8, 2011.

[25] Interview with Democratic Party fundraiser with experience in federal campaigns, July 21, 2011.

[26] Pew Research Center, "Search and Email Still the Most Popular Online Activities," August 9, 2011, http://pewresearch.org/pubs/2079/-email-internet-search, accessed August 25, 2011.

[27] Interview with Jennifer Stolp, Vice President for Fundraising, Campaign Solutions, July 8, 2011.

[28] Interview with Doug Jaraczewski, President and Founder, Campaign Finance Group, June 30, 2011.

[29] Interview with Doug Jaraczewski, President and Founder, Campaign Finance Group, June 30, 2011.

[30] Interview with Scott Dworkin, Founder and CEO, Bulldog Finance Group, July 5, 2011.

[31] Interview with Jennifer Stolp, Vice President for Fundraising, Campaign Solutions, July 8, 2011.

[32] Interview with Democratic Party fundraiser with experience in House races, October 13, 2011.

[33] Steve O'Hear, "John Edwards's Campaign Enters Second Life," ZDNet, February 14, 2007, http://www.zdnet.com/blog/social/john-edwards-campaign-enters-second-life/91, accessed August 25, 2011.

[34] Interview with Jennifer Stolp, Vice President for Fundraising, Campaign Solutions, July 8, 2011.

[35] Interview with Democratic Party fundraiser with experience in congressional campaigns, June 16, 2011.

[36] Interview with Scott Dworkin, Founder and CEO, Bulldog Finance Group, July 5, 2011.

[37] Interview with Doug Jaraczewski, President and Founder, Campaign Finance Group, June 30, 2011.

[38] Interview with Neal Harrington, President, Harrington Forward Thinking, August 8, 2011.

[39] Interview with Democratic Party fundraiser with experience in congressional campaigns, June 16, 2011.

[40] Interview with Peter Pasi, Executive Vice President, Emotive LLC, August 5, 2011.

[41] Interview with Neal Harrington, Harrington Forward Thinking, August 8, 2011.

[42] Interview with Jennifer Stolp, Vice President for Fundraising, Campaign Solutions, July 8, 2011.

5

How Members of Congress Build Their Fundraising Coalitions

Each candidate for office faces a fundraising puzzle. He or she needs money in order to mount an effective campaign, so how should that money be raised? Just as there is not one single potential source of money, there is not one single best strategy for raising it. A candidate's most effective fundraising strategy will depend on two sets of factors: the factors that motivate people who might contribute, and the characteristics of the candidate that could prompt contributions.

In Chapter 2, I discussed varying theoretical explanations of why individuals might contribute to political campaigns and causes. In this chapter, I begin to examine the available data to determine which theory – or combination of theories – best explain the data on individual giving that we observe in the U.S. political campaign environment.

There are two major sources of data available on this question, neither of which is perfect. The first is data on contributions reported to the Federal Election Commission (FEC) as part of the legally-mandated reporting process. Most scholars consider these data to be accurate and well-reported, in contrast to the inconsistent and nearly useless reporting data that were collected prior to the 1970s. The second source is survey data from the National Election Studies, the most extensive and longest-running series of surveys on political questions available to political scientists. The FEC data directly measure contributions, but include no information on contributor motivations; the NES survey data allow us to get a clearer picture of motivation, but contain little information on who contributed how much to which campaign. In this chapter I focus on the FEC reporting data on contributions; in Chapter 6 I turn to survey data from the National Election Studies.

The FEC data have the advantage of being publicly accessible and reported in a standardized format. Campaigns must report data on the contributions they receive from a number of different sources, including the candidate himself or herself, parties, political action committees (PACs) and individual contributors. Campaigns and other political committees also itemize their expenditures, debts, and borrowing patterns, although this information is less useful for the purposes of studying contributions. Campaigns file reports at regular intervals throughout the campaign cycle, and they correct errors by filing amendments if necessary. Finally, the FEC assigns each candidate a unique identification number so that candidates can be tracked across campaigns in multiple years.

The FEC data do have their drawbacks, however. The most obvious of these is that in contrast to survey data, we only observe contributors' actions – not the reasons behind those actions. For example, a donor may be the CEO of Amalgamated Widgets, Inc. and may contribute cash to a candidate who supports the interests of Amalgamated Widgets. But we do not know for certain that the contribution was motivated by these material concerns. This is only an inference, albeit a reasonably well supported one.

Second, campaigns are not required to itemize individual contributions below the level of $200. For contributions above this amount, campaigns must collect contributor names, addresses, and occupations, but for the smallest contributors this information is not required. Some campaigns collect this information anyway – in the early 1990s, Representative Romano Mazzoli (D-KY) refused to accept campaign contributions of larger than $100, and reported each contribution in as much detail as he could, meticulously itemizing the names and occupations of even the smallest donors. But this is an exception, not the rule.

Although we have information on the aggregate amounts candidates collect from small contributors, therefore, we do not have consistent detailed information on who these contributors are. This makes imputing their motives more difficult.

The approach I take in this chapter therefore relies on the behavior of individuals in the aggregate. Fortunately, the FEC provides summary data files for each congressional race reaching back to the 1980 cycle that provide good information on aggregate contribution levels from individuals, PACs, and parties. From 1990 to 2006, the FEC summary files distinguish those who contribute below $200 from other contributors, allowing researchers to determine how much money each candidate collected from contributions below $200.[1]

As the literature on interest groups shows, the contributions of individuals to a collective effort are dependent not just on supply-side (individual-level) factors, but also on demand-side (candidate level) variables. Interest groups succeed or fail not only because of the differing willingness of their supporters to contribute, but also because of the divergent strategies of the "political entrepreneurs" who lead them. Like interest group organizers, candidates and campaigns may choose to more aggressively solicit one type of group over another (PACs over individuals, for example). If one's district has a lower per capita income than is typical, one might find that individuals are prepared to give less, and a candidate might choose to ramp up his or her PAC solicitation in response.

This candidate specialization works in our favor because variation allows us to better perceive patterns and relationships in the data. In particular, as discussed in Chapter 2, contributors with "purposive" motivations are more likely to contribute to campaigns and causes with clear ideological goals. Candidates whose goals are clearly defined and principled, therefore, ought to have a comparative advantage in fundraising with respect to purposive donors, and should focus their efforts more on purposive contributors and less on material or solidary contributors.

In general, therefore, I presume a model in which the relationship between contributions and fundraising is interactive, but in which a candidate that has a comparative advantage with one aspect of fundraising will tend to rely more heavily on that aspect than a candidate who has a comparative advantage in another aspect of fundraising. This is because a rational candidate can be expected to choose the least-cost means of achieving his or her goals. Focusing on one's area of comparative advantage is "cheaper" than the alternatives.

This model may seem more familiar if we discuss the area of PAC contributions – the focus of most campaign finance literature in political science. Reformers and scholars alike have long recognized that candidates from districts in which (for example) agribusiness dominates the employment picture are more likely to collect more PAC contributions from agribusiness interests; members of Congress from districts in which the insurance industry is strong likewise collect more money from insurance company PACs. Reformers allege that these relationships are clear evidence of the corruption endemic in the system. The website OpenSecrets.org notes that Republican Representative William Flores of Texas collected over $340,000 from PACs during the 2010 cycle, and that "an array of oil and gas industry groups including Anadarko Petroleum, ConocoPhillips, ExxonMobil, and Marathon Oil were among those that kicked in."[2] We are led to infer that these groups have purchased Flores's allegiance.

But this presumption rests heavily on a supply-side view of things. It may instead be the case that members of Congress from agribusiness-dominated districts simply have a comparative advantage in collecting agribusiness contributions. Flores, for example, represents a Texas district south of Dallas in which energy is a significant employer. Furthermore, Flores himself is a former energy company executive, whose connections presumably make it easier for him to raise money from this source. Flores may simply be focusing on his area of comparative advantage; demand-side factors, in other words, may also come into play.

The same logic of comparative advantage might apply to PACs in general versus other sorts of contributions. Herb Kohl, the longtime Democratic senator from Wisconsin whose campaign slogan, "Nobody's Senator but Yours," highlighted his refusal to accept PAC donations, had a clear advantage vis a vis other candidates in an alternate source of funds: his own personal wealth. Because of his circumstances, Kohl found it easier to reject PAC funding and pay much of the cost of his campaigns out of his own pocket. More commonly, those with powerful committee positions are more likely to be in a position to collect funds from PACs whose interests lie with the committee. In 2010, Representative Barney Frank (D-MA), who at the time was head of the House Financial Services Committee, collected over \$340,000 from interests related to "securities and investment," according to OpenSecrets.org.[3] It is reasonable to suspect that Frank's position at the head of this powerful committee gave him a comparative advantage in fundraising from banking interests.

Reformers decry these PAC interests as material, and no doubt they often are. Certainly, large banks and securities firms would not refuse any favors they are offered from key members of Congress. The logic of the "demand side" and of comparative advantage might also apply, however, in the (plausible) case that PAC incentives are solidary. Perhaps connected firms instruct PAC directors to contribute so that CEOs will get invited to prestigious events. It is also possible that a solidary motive could be connected with a manner of coercion by candidates –PACs may get solicited from a known representative and are unwilling to sour their relationship with that person for the sake of saving \$500 or \$1000. In any case, members of Congress often appear to make use of their own particular advantages in pursuing avenues of fundraising.

Using the FEC Data to test the "Comparative Advantage" Model

The Federal Election Commission data provide an excellent opportunity for testing the extent to which congressional fundraising patterns conform to this expectation regarding candidates' comparative advantages. Below I describe in detail the way in which I use the data to test this expectation.

Dependent Variable: The Proportion of Funds Raised from Individuals

In the aggregate, we ought to see candidates raising disproportionately more funds from sources with which they have a comparative advantage. The FEC data do not allow for a perfect test of the theories of contributor motivations outlined in Chapter 2, but they allow at least a partial examination.

The first task at hand is to identify (within the limits of what the FEC data will allow) exactly what we should be trying to explain – the dependent variable. This is important and not necessarily obvious. Most previous studies have focused on whether or not candidates received contributions from various different kinds of PACs. This allows us to test for the possibility that PACs influence congressional voting behavior (or other congressional activity), but cannot address the questions regarding fundraising strategy that we need to answer here.

A second group of studies has focused on the dollar amounts raised by candidates, either as a whole or by category (PACs, individuals, party funds, etc.). These studies can gain insight into the factors behind success in overall fundraising, a subject close to, but not the same as, the issue of most interest here. Overall fundraising success is a good sign of a candidate's popularity, renown, and electoral viability, as well as of his or her dedication and skill at fundraising itself. It is not necessarily a good measure of a candidate's comparative advantage in fundraising from one source over another.

Consider a comparison between two candidates to determine which one is better at raising money from individual contributors. If the two candidates raise money only from individual contributors, their aggregate fundraising totals are indeed a good measure of their prowess in this area. When different sources of funds enter into the equation, however, the total amount raised becomes less useful. The candidate who is less adept at raising money from individuals may make up for this deficiency by, say, raising money from Political Action

Committees. The two candidates' total amount raised may be the same, but it obscures the true difference between the two candidates. In fact, this is what existing studies have found. Those who have examined candidates' aggregate fundraising totals conclude that some factors, such as candidate ideology, that may make a difference in a candidate's comparative advantages, make little or no difference in aggregate fundraising (McCarty, Poole, & Rosenthal 2006).

A better way to measure individual candidates' comparative advantages with different fundraising audiences is to focus on the proportion of funds candidates raise from each major source. A candidate that is particularly good at raising individual contributions should be expected to raise more of his or her funds from individuals than a candidate who is better at soliciting PACs. Similarly, a candidate that has a great deal of personal wealth may be more likely to rely on that source of funds; a candidate with close ties to the national party organization might rely on more party money than is typical.

In the rest of the chapter, therefore, I focus on the money raised from a particular source *as a proportion of the overall total amount raised* as my dependent variable. In particular, most of my analysis focuses on the proportion raised from individual contributions. I narrow my focus to this single source because in practice, the majority of campaigns rely on two major sources: PACs and individual contributions. Party money and personal spending make up a very small proportion of overall campaign spending. The proportion raised from individual contributions is in most cases simply the mirror image of the proportion raised from Political Action Committees, so to run separate analyses with both proportions would be redundant. Those variables that have a negative effect on the proportion raised from individuals therefore have a positive effect on the proportion raised from PACs, and vice versa.

Now that the dependent variable is established, I turn to a discussion of the measurement of the causal variables. The key causal variables ought to be designed to test – as well as is practicable – the theories of why people contribute developed in Chapter 2.

Solidary

Considering the data we have available from the FEC, the most problematic category of contribution is the solidary category. Recall the predictions from Chapter 2 about solidary contributors:

People are more likely to contribute if they enjoy the company of like minded others.

People are more likely to contribute if they are more embedded within social networks.

People are more likely to contribute if they have been asked to contribute by someone they know.

The first two of these predictions concern characteristics of the contributors (the supply side), while the second might be viewed as concerning the demand side (whether the candidate is well-connected to potential contributors). The difficulty is not on the demand side – indeed, it is easy to think of good measurements of a candidate or member of Congress's sociability or "networked-ness." The most obvious might be a member's level of higher education. As one fundraiser told me, it is *de rigueur* to begin a campaign by soliciting "brothers and sisters and whatever. You've got everyone they went to college with, everyone they went to law school with, everyone they've been in business with, everyone they used to be in business with, everyone they interned with at one point – everyone they personally know."[4] This primary circle of contributors is larger if a candidate has more connections through informal alumni networks from law schools, business schools, or other institutions of higher learning.

But the operationalization of a solidary incentive falters when we come to the supply side. It is impossible to tell from aggregating fundraising statistics which contributors represent solidary contributors and which represent material or purposive contributors. We usually think of solidary motives as applying to individuals, but as I discussed above, PACs, too, may give for solidary reasons. Similarly, a large contributor may give because he or she wants something material from an elected official, or that contributor may have wanted to support a candidate who happened to be a friend from law school. No simple marker in the FEC data will distinguish a solidary contributor or group of contributors from a material or purposive individual or group. I therefore leave the testing for solidary contributions to the next chapter, which focuses on survey data.

Material

It is, however, possible to use the FEC data to get a better analytical handle on material and purposive contributions. Recall the predictions from Chapter 2 about material incentives:

People are more likely to contribute if they have occupations that make a collective good more like a private good.

People are more likely to contribute if they have received money or gifts from those organizing to provide the collective good.

This pair of predictions includes both a supply side (the occupations of the contributors), and a demand side (the position of the recipients). On the demand side, material contributions are more likely if a candidate is in a position to do meaningful favors for contributors. This, first of all, suggests that material contributors are likely to give disproportionately to incumbents, since those who are in Congress are better positioned to do favors than those who are – as yet – without any official position. Second, those who are members of the governing party may have more clout than those in the opposition – especially in the House of Representatives. And finally, those who hold key positions in Congress – those who sit on important committees, for example, have more power to move legislation, shape bills, engage in oversight, or influence the regulatory process than members who do not hold these positions. Candidates who have one or more of these characteristics, therefore, are likely to have a comparative advantage in raising material contributions over those who do not hold such positions.

So much for the demand side. Considering the predictions above, which identifiable contributor groups are likely to be material contributors? Here we have a better answer than for solidary contributors. Political Action Committees, while they may have multiple motives, from solidary to purposive, are more likely to be disproportionately material in their focus than any other contributor group. The vast majority of PACs are launched by business organizations (individual businesses as well as trade associations), and these can be expected to further the interests of their affiliated business – one of the key material benefits outlined above in Chapter 2. The majority of previous political science studies on PACs have treated them as materially interested (see, e.g. Hall and Wayman 1990). Finally, although some small number of PACs does seem to behave purposively (some seem not to give disproportionately to incumbents, for example), these are the exceptions. When looking at a candidate's fundraising totals in general, therefore, the material tendency ought to dominate other tendencies in the case of Political Action Committees.

Purposive and Expressive

As Chapter 2 explains, predictions about purposive and expressive incentives are varied:

Purposive Incentive Predictions (Clark & Wilson 1961)

> People are more likely to contribute if they have strong preferences regarding goals.
> People are more likely to contribute to organizations with clearly defined goals.
> People are more likely to contribute if they feel they can be influential in the accomplishment of a goal or sub-goal.

Expressive Incentives, General Predictions (Salisbury 1969)

> People will contribute if the act of contributing provides an intrinsic benefit to them.
> People's contributions should not depend on whether they feel (or possess) any causal agency towards the provision of a collective or public good.

Socially Defined Expressive Incentives Predictions (Knoke & Wood 1981; Andreoni 1989, 1990)

> People are more likely to contribute the more socialized they are to respect common values associated with the political process and political goals.
> People are more likely to contribute to candidates and causes in which basic values are more directly invoked or implicated, and less likely to contribute to candidates and causes that are more remote from basic values.

Emotionally Defined Expressive Incentives Predictions (Marcus 2002; Brader 2006)

> People who are affectively engaged with politics – particularly those whom politics makes more fearful – will be more likely to contribute.

Most of the predictions concerning intangible purposive and expressive incentives concern characteristics of individuals that cannot be observed at the level of the FEC data available. A contributor's strength of preferences, the level of intrinsic benefit a contribution represents, and how socialized he or she is are characteristics that are not observable with the data at hand. However, there are a number of demand side factors that might be measurable. A campaign can decide whether to invoke basic values, for example, and take clear and well-defined positions. A campaign can also work to instill feelings of causal agency among contributors by setting a series of intermediate goals or challenges. Finally, if a campaign is expected to be a close race, we should expect more purposive contributions because it then becomes more likely that an individual will affect the outcome of the election.

The closeness of the race is easily measured: the final victory margin can serve as a reasonable proxy for how close potential contributors expected the race to be in the late stages of the campaign. Whether a campaign sets intermediate goals is more difficult to determine, especially in a large dataset with campaigns dating back to the 1980s. The closest thing to a measurement of this factor is whether a candidate faced a primary challenge or not – a natural "intermediate goal." This variable is certainly imperfect, but it will have to serve for our purposes.

Finally comes the question of how to measure the clarity and value-laden content of campaign messages. Here I choose to use a measure of incumbent ideology generated by Keith Poole and Howard Rosenthal (Poole & Rosenthal 1997). Poole and Rosenthal's analysis of congressional voting patterns over more than two centuries show that most congressional votes – especially in recent years – can be explained by a single dimension of liberal-conservative ideology. Poole and Rosenthal's analytic process generates a variable that allows us to compare incumbents – pinpointing which are the most conservative, which are the most moderate, and what the relative 'distance' is between members of Congress.

Extreme liberal or conservative ideology serves as a good approximation of message clarity and value content. Those at the opposite ends of the political spectrum are most likely to explain their positions in stark and principled terms. Moderates, who by their nature are open to compromise, are naturally disadvantaged in terms of clarity and force of message.

It is true that this does not necessarily have to be the case. In calling for a party system with more clarity and precision, the American Political Science Association stressed in a 1950 report that "clarification of party policy" need not "cause the parties to differ more fundamentally or more sharply than they have in the past" (American Political Science Association 1950, p. 2). On occasion, we do hear of a vocal and principled moderate, but these politicians are rare. More commonly, activists on either side attack moderates for being unprincipled. Independent candidate George Wallace made this point famously by saying of Democrats and Republicans "Put 'em all in the same sack, shake 'em up. I don't care which one comes out, you stick him back in – because there isn't a dime's worth of difference in them" (Lesher 1994, p. 367). Furthermore, survey data show that the farther apart parties are in their congressional voting patterns, the easier it is for Americans to identify differences between them. National Election Studies data show that in 1972, at the low ebb of congressional party polarization, less than a majority of Americans (47 percent) said that they thought that there were "important differences in what the Democratic and Republican Parties stand for." By 2008, with congressional parties farther apart in ideology than at any time in generations, that figure had increased to 78 percent. In this respect, therefore, ideological distance does appear to generate clarity.

A summary of the key variables to be measured in the Federal Election Commission data appears below, organized by supply-side and demand-side factors.

Demand Side

Extremism: Incumbents' ideology score as measured by the first dimension DWNominate score, calculated by Poole and Rosenthal based on congressional voting records (see their website at www.voteview.com). I "fold" this measure at the median for each Congress, so that those who are more extreme are the ones that are more distant from the median member of the Congress of which they are members.

Years in office: The longer the incumbent has been in office, the more fundraising connections he or she may have, the more skilled at fundraising he or she may be, and the more seniority he or she may have accumulated in Congress.

Total receipts: A campaign's fundraising strategies may differ for a low-cost campaign versus a high-cost campaign. The total aggregate receipts are a good representation of the campaign's overall cost.

Primary loss: Those incumbents who lose primaries are expected to raise less money because they do not have a general election campaign to run. They also may raise money in different proportions because primary campaign fundraising may differ from general election fundraising.

Committee memberships: Incumbents' membership on the five so-called "power committees," Rules, Appropriations, Ways and Means, Commerce, and Budget. Members of these committees may be systematically more capable of raising money from Political Action Committees due to their proximity to potential material rewards.

Supply Side

District median income (logged): The median income of the district may affect the wealth available for the incumbent to raise from individuals, with less wealthy districts making fundraising comparatively more difficult.

Closeness of the race: Individuals may contribute more money to incumbents in close races than to incumbents who are set to win handily due to a purposive desire to affect the outcome of the election. PACs, on the other hand, may be more likely to contribute to a "sure thing" so as to increase the probability of securing a material benefit.

Democrats vs. Republicans: Party affiliation may be both a supply-side factor and a demand-side factor. Members of the majority party may have more power and therefore may have a greater comparative advantage with material contributors. Democrats also tend to win more support from lower-income voters, and may therefore be less likely to succeed in raising money from larger individual contributors than Republicans.

Data Analysis

My technique is multi-level (sometimes called "hierarchical") modeling. The details of this complex procedure appear in the chapter appendix. In brief, multilevel modeling allows for partial pooling of results for different subsets of the data to account for non-independence of cases within subsets, and for different effects of the key variables within these subsets. I conduct separate multilevel analyses with two different dependent variables: the proportion raised by each member of Congress from all individuals, and the proportion raised from individuals contributing below $200. These proportions are modeled as being related in a linear way to the independent variables. Results are reported in Table 5.1.

**Table 5.1: Multilevel Model: Effects of Extremism
on Proportion of Funds Raised from Individuals**

Dependent Variable	Proportion from all individuals (1984-2010)	Proportion from those contributing less than $200 (1990-2010)
Demand Side		
Extremism	.10 (.04)	.06 (.03)
Years in office	.00 (.00)	.00 (.00)
Total receipts (logged)	.06 (.00)	.01 (.00)
Primary loss	.06 (.02)	.00 (.01)
Rules Committee	-.02 (.01)	.00 (.01)
Appropriations Committee	.02 (.01)	-.01 (.01)
Ways and Means Committee	-.09 (.01)	-.02 (.01)
Commerce Committee	-.07 (.01)	-.02 (.01)
Budget Committee	.02 (.01)	.00 (.00)
Supply Side		
District median income (logged)	.04 (.01)	.01 (.01)
Percent of vote received	.00 (.00)	.00 (.00)
Democrat	-.09 (.01)	-.07 (.01)
Intercept	-.73 (.12)	.04 (.11)
SD for member intercepts	.12	.08
SD for state intercepts	.04	.01
SD for state slopes	.05	.04
Group correlation parameter for states	-.34	.47
SD for party intercept	.00	.00
SD for party slopes	.05	.04
Group correlation parameter for party	.00	.00
SD for election cycle intercepts	.03	.05
SD for election cycle slopes	.06	.04
Group correlation parameter for election cycle	-.75	-.25

Residual	.09	.06
Deviance	-8923.6	-10463
Total observations	5,535	4.324
Members of Congress	1,187	1045
States	50	50
Election Cycles	14	11
Parties	2	2

The first column of Table 5.1 shows that a number of both supply and demand-side factors affect the proportion of funds that candidates raise from individuals. Extremism matters: if a candidate moves from the median to a point two standard deviations away on the extremism measure, he or she changes the proportion of funds raised from individuals by approximately five percent. This amount is equivalent to over $57,000 in 2012 dollars for the average campaign, or about one-third of a standard deviation in the percent raised from individuals. Candidates with a clear and pointed message do appear to do better with individual contributors, other things being equal, as the purposive theory suggests.

Other demand side factors also play a role: a candidate's total receipts, whether the candidate won the primary, and certain committee memberships (Ways and Means and Commerce, especially) all affect the proportion of individual funds that candidates raise. On the supply side, district median income and a candidate's party identification also have effects. As expected, the higher the median income of a district, the higher the proportion of funds candidates collect from individual contributors. Democrats collect a smaller share of their money from individuals than Republicans do, perhaps because Republican voters tend to have higher incomes than Democratic Party voters.

Extremism also appears to affect Democratic campaigns in a different way than Republican campaigns. As Figure 5.1 shows, the effect of extremism for Democrats is more than twice as steep (.13) than it is for Republicans (.07). In the figure, the lines represent the estimated effect of extremism, holding other factors constant; each grey dot represents a campaign. The steeper slope of the line for Democrats reflects the greater effect. The explanation for this difference is not obvious considering the data at hand. Republican campaigns collect a larger proportion of their funds from individuals than do Democratic campaigns, so it may be that Republican voters, wealthier on average, are simply more willing to give money to their co-partisans regardless of their level of extremism.

Figure 5.1: Effect of Extremism on Democratic and Republican Party Campaigns; House Incumbents, 1984-2010, Proportion of Funds Raised from All Individuals as the Dependent Variable (y-axis)

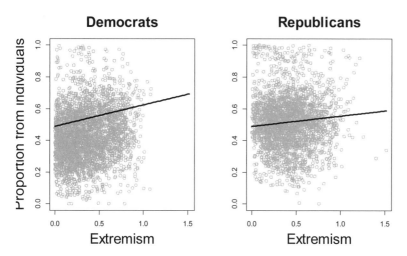

When the dependent variable is restricted to only the smallest contributions, the difference between Democrats and Republicans persists, and even widens slightly. The effect of many other variables besides extremism, including district income and committee memberships drop to marginal or no significance. Extremism remains an important explanatory variable, indicating that for those contributing less than $200, the candidate's ideological position makes a clear difference. Variation in the proportion of funds collected from small individual donations can be explained by candidate extremism, and little else.

The effect of extremism also appears to be changing over time. Figure 5.2 shows the estimated effect of extremism (the slope of such lines as appear in Figure 5.1) in every election cycle from 1984 to 2010. A curious pattern emerges here. The effect of extremism was large in the 1980s and early 1990s, small in the mid-1990s, and larger again from 2000 to 2006. In the 2008 and 2010 cycles, however, the effect is indistinguishable from zero. The increasingly strong effect for extremism from 2000 to 2006 is consistent with the hypothesis that new technologies – in particular the rise of the internet – have interacted with

Figure 5.2: Effects of Extremism on Giving from Individuals, 1984-2010; Predicted Effect of Extremism Has Decreased as Polarization Has Increased

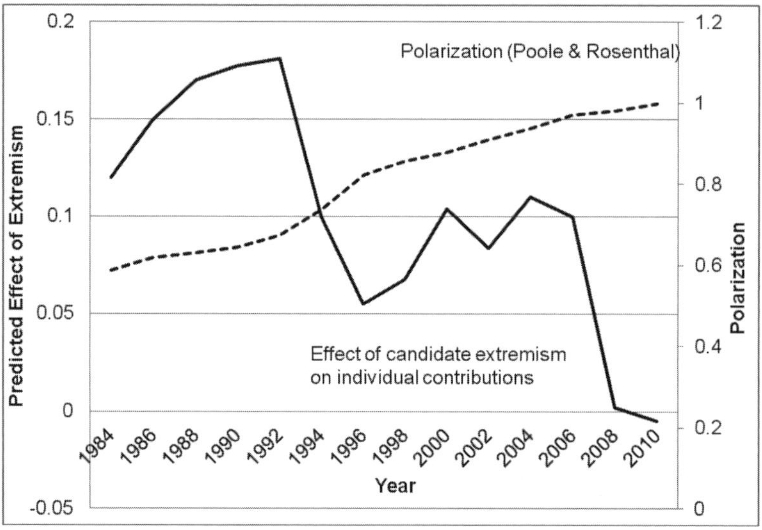

candidate extremism, making it easier for ideologically motivated potential contributors to find attractive candidates. This does not explain the absence of the effect in the last two cycles however.

This is a particularly puzzling finding in light of the increasingly polarized political environment. Figure 5.2 also graphs the level of polarization in Congress, as measured by Poole and Rosenthal as the distance between the ideological score of the two parties' median members.[5] In this more polarized U.S. political environment, we might expect extremism to have a greater rather than a smaller effect on contribution patterns, due to the increase in clear, distinct messaging from candidates.

Survey data on how Americans – especially campaign contributors – view the political parties confirm that U.S. citizens see the messages of party elites as increasingly clear and distinct. Figure 5.3 shows the percentage of respondents from 1952 to 2008 who say there are "important differences" between the parties. Those seeing such differences have increased substantially since 2008 – especially among contributors. Now over 90 percent of those who give money to

Figure 5.3: Over Time, The Percentage of Those Who See "Important Differences" Between the Political Parties Has Increased

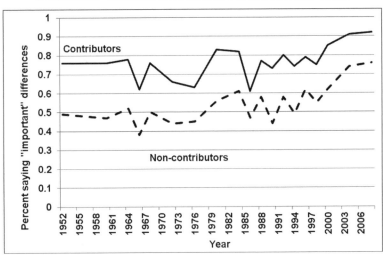

Source: American National Election Studies.

campaigns and parties see important differences between the two sides. In this environment, contributors might be expected to seek out those who reliably conform to the party line, rather than those who blur the differences between the parties.

Non-Linear Effects and the Divergence of Campaign Strategies

One plausible explanation for the failure of the model described above to identify a significant effect for extremism in recent years is that the way in which extremism figures into campaign strategies has changed over the decades for which data are available. As noted above, the model assumes that the effect of extremism is linear: that is, if a candidate moves a set distance from the median ideological position, he or she receives a constant increase in the proportion of individual contributions. It may be that in the current polarized environment, the effect has become non-linear. A candidate's proportion of individual contributions may not change unless and until he or she becomes quite extreme, after which point the proportion of individual contributions soars. This is consistent with the idea that prospective donors seek out candidates that maintain a clear ideological orthodoxy across issues, and (conversely) with the theory that such candidates will find they have a comparative advantage in soliciting contributions in small amounts from individuals.

To test for this possibility, I restrict the data set to the 2008 and 2010 election cycles and estimate two simple logistic regression models. Logistic regression is a standard technique for estimating non-linear effects. I define my dependent variables in terms of the dependent variables in the above model, but here I create two dichotomous (zero-one) variables that are coded zero unless a campaign is in the 75th percentile or above in the proportion of individual contributions or the proportion of contributions below \$200, respectively. The models therefore estimate the probability that a campaign will be unusually reliant on individual (or the smallest individual) contributions.[6] The key independent variable remains "extremism," as defined above, and I retain controls for total receipts, percent of the vote received, district income, party affiliation, committee memberships, and whether the candidate lost the primary.[7]

The control variables behave more or less as they do in the models above. For individual contributions as a whole (but not for the smallest contributions), key committee memberships diminish the probability of disproportionate reliance on individual contributions. In districts with higher median incomes, candidates are more likely to rely on such contributions. The longer a representative has served in Congress, the less likely he or she is to collect a large amount from individuals (and, therefore, the more likely he or she is to rely on PAC contributions).

The effect of extremism is striking. Whereas the linear model above found little or no relationship for 2008 and 2010 between the proportion of funds received from individuals and a candidate's ideological distance from the center, the non-linear models for those same years find a clear connection. A candidate's probability of falling in the 75th percentile or above in his or her reliance on individual contributions quadruples (from 0.10 to 0.43) as we move from the median to the most extreme ideological position (see Figure 5.4).

When the dependent variable is restricted to focus only on contributions below \$200, the effect is even clearer. A candidate's probability of falling at or above the 75th percentile leaps from 0.04 to 0.48 as we move from the median to the most extreme ideological position (Figure 5.5). In both cases, these relationships are very unlikely to have occurred by chance, as the 95 percent confidence intervals represented by the dotted lines in the figures show.[8]

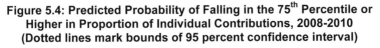

Figure 5.4: Predicted Probability of Falling in the 75th Percentile or Higher in Proportion of Individual Contributions, 2008-2010 (Dotted lines mark bounds of 95 percent confidence interval)

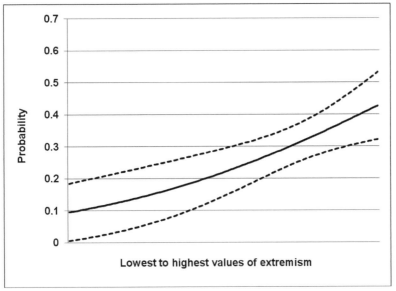

This clear nonlinear effect for 2008 and 2010 suggests that candidate strategies – and along with them, individual giving patterns – have diverged in recent election cycles. Candidates that have a clear advantage with individual contributors are those who hold the most extreme positions; other candidates have fewer advantages with individual contributors. An incumbent with an ideological position at his or her political party's median, such as Bill Pascrell (D-NJ) in 2010, changes his or her individual fundraising very little when compared to a member of Congress at the center of the chamber, such as Collin Peterson (D-MN). Only when a candidate moves to the far ideological edges of his or her party does the probability of relying heavily on individual contributions jump.

When did this nonlinear effect emerge? Similar logistic regression models from previous cycles reveal that significant nonlinearity exists in the early 2000s, but disappears by the early 1990s. The nonlinear effect of a candidate's ideological position on his or her fundraising coalition coincided with the growth in the number of individual contributions that occurred in the last 15 years. This discovery is consistent with the

Figure 5.5: Predicted Probability of Falling in the 75th Percentile or Higher in Proportion of Small (<$200) Contributions, 2008-2010 (Dotted lines mark bounds of 95 percent confidence interval)

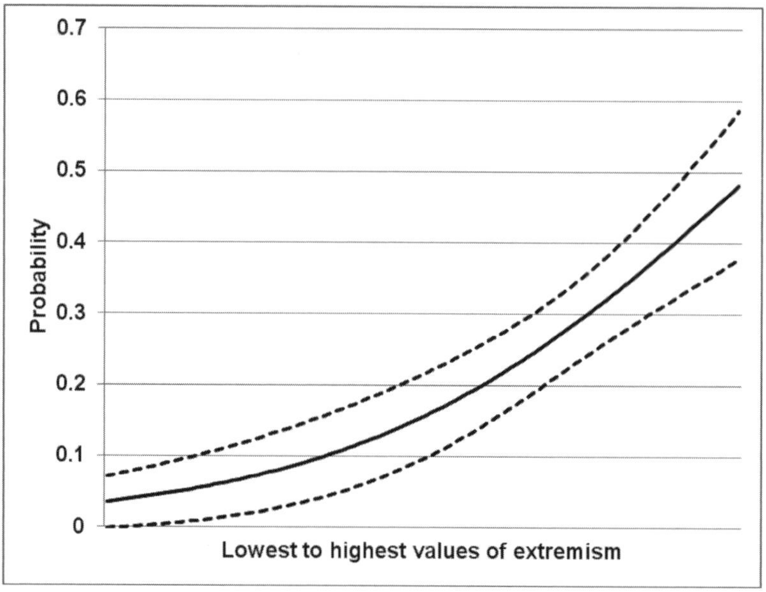

intriguing finding by Ray LaRaja and David Wiltse that the proportion of ideological givers has increased since 2002, perhaps as a result of the strategic mobilization of ideologues by candidates (LaRaja and Wiltse 2012). This may be further evidence that extreme candidates have become increasingly adept at making use of their comparative advantage with ideological donors.

A caveat is in order about this non-linear effect. Because I modeled the 2008 and 2010 data in a non-linear way as a result of a curious puzzle in a previous analysis of the same data, a critic might argue that I have insufficiently tested this new model. It is true that to fully test this model of increasing non-linearity in the construction of fundraising coalitions, it would be best to have additional data that were not in hand when the model was developed (see King, Keohane, & Verba 1994 for a discussion of this issue). Data that are precisely comparable, however, will only emerge after several more election cycles. Future testing will undoubtedly refine the analysis presented here, but the data currently available are necessarily limited.

Conclusion

The tests in this chapter using Federal Election Commission data confirm the purposive theory of contributing, and also support the material explanation for some types of gifts. Individual contributors – and small individual contributors who can hope to gain little from their sub-$200 contributions – make up a proportionately larger share of the fundraising pie for candidates who are far from the ideological median. Incumbents who are nearer to the median and who hold key positions on powerful congressional committees are more likely to raise most of their money from Political Action Committees, which are more likely to be motivated by material concerns. Because candidates can be expected to focus on their areas of personal comparative advantage in their fundraising strategies, these differences likely reflect real advantages and disadvantages that candidates face in attracting different types of contributors.

Finally, one drawback of the analysis in this chapter is that it focuses solely on incumbents running for reelection. This was a necessary restriction because the key measure of ideology – the DW Nominate score – is only available for incumbents because it is based on voting records in Congress. Challenger fundraising is likely quite different because incumbents all have clear advantages in raising money from materially-oriented donors. A potential contributor who expects something in return for a contribution can reasonably assume that his or her chances are better with a sitting member of Congress than with a newcomer whose prospects are uncertain. This presumption finds support in the donation patterns of PACs, who contribute overwhelmingly to incumbents.

Figure 3.4 above hints at some of the potential differences between incumbents and challengers by plotting the standard deviation of the proportion collected from individuals for incumbent and challenger campaigns over time. The standard deviation is a measure of the variability of a measure – the larger the standard deviation, the larger the variability.

As Figure 3.4 shows, all types of candidates except incumbents have collected an increasingly variable proportion of their funds from individuals since 1984. One way to interpret this finding might be to say that it reflects an increasing tendency for non-incumbents to specialize in one particular type of fundraising or another. If the analysis in this chapter is correct, this specialization can be expected to be related to candidates' areas of comparative advantage. Those who have clearer and more distinct ideological positions should focus more on small individual contributions; those without such positions should focus on other areas of fundraising. The true effect of ideological extremism on fundraising is probably larger than that discussed in this chapter. For challengers, ideological extremism may represent a critical opportunity to raise funds that might be tougher to raise otherwise.

Multilevel Model

In this chapter I estimate a multilevel model that generates parameter estimates by partially pooling information from four groups for which effects of extremism may be correlated: individual members of Congress (running in multiple cycles), states, election cycles, and political parties (see Gelman & Hill 2007). I allow slopes and intercepts for the key "extremism" variable to vary by state, election cycle, and party, and allow intercepts to vary for each individual member of Congress. There are a number of different ways to express a multilevel model, but one way of representing this model is contained in the following set of equations. First, the main model contains separate constant terms and separate slope terms for the extremism variable (E).

$$y_i \sim N(\alpha_{j(i)} + \alpha_{k(i)} + \alpha_{l(i)} + \alpha_{m(i)} + X_i^0 \beta^0 + E_i B_k + E_i B_l + E_i B_m) \; for \; i = 1, ..., n$$

where i represents each case, an individual campaign in an individual year for an individual incumbent. Individual-level coefficients are modeled for all independent variables, so that $X_i^0 \beta^0$ represents a matrix of predictors (including extremism) multiplied by regression coefficients. Intercepts vary for each member of Congress (a modeling decision made based on the supposition that campaigns run by the same member in multiple cycles are not independent of one another), so that:

$$\alpha_{j[i]} \sim N(\mu_{\alpha j}, \sigma_{\alpha j}^2) \; for \; j = 1, ..., J$$

where J=1022 separate members of Congress. For states and election cycles, separate intercepts and slopes are modeled jointly. In the case of states:

$$\begin{pmatrix} \alpha_k \\ B_k \end{pmatrix} \sim N\left(\begin{pmatrix} \mu_{\alpha k} \\ \mu_{B k} \end{pmatrix} \begin{pmatrix} \sigma_{\alpha k}^2 & \rho_k \sigma_{\alpha k} \sigma_{B k} \\ \rho_k \sigma_{\alpha k} \sigma_{B k} & \sigma_{\alpha k}^2 \end{pmatrix} \right) \; for \; k = 1, ..., K$$

for K= 50 states. The ρ_k represents a between-group correlation parameter. Similarly, for election cycles,

$$\begin{pmatrix} \alpha_l \\ B_l \end{pmatrix} \sim N(\begin{pmatrix} \mu_{\alpha l} \\ \mu_{Bl} \end{pmatrix} \begin{pmatrix} \sigma^2_{\alpha l} & \rho_l \sigma_{\alpha l} \sigma_{Bl} \\ \rho_l \sigma_{\alpha l} \sigma_{Bl} & \sigma^2_{\alpha l} \end{pmatrix}) \ for \ l = 1, ..., L$$

for L=11 election cycles. Finally, for parties,

$$\begin{pmatrix} \alpha_m \\ B_m \end{pmatrix} \sim N(\begin{pmatrix} \mu_{\alpha m} \\ \mu_{Bm} \end{pmatrix} \begin{pmatrix} \sigma^2_{\alpha m} & \rho_m \sigma_{\alpha m} \sigma_{Bm} \\ \rho_m \sigma_{\alpha m} \sigma_{Bm} & \sigma^2_{\alpha m} \end{pmatrix}) \ for \ m = 1, 2$$

for two parties. Table 3.1 reports coefficients from the main equation, as well as standard deviation parameters for group intercepts and slopes where applicable.

---

[1] After 2006, summary the preliminary data files available at fec.gov do not separate the below-$200 contributors from other individual contributors.

[2] Eric Pianin, Jennifer DePaul, and Michelle Hirsch, "Congressional Freshmen Saddled with Debt Turn to PACs," OpenSecrets.org, April 14, 2011, http://www.opensecrets.org/news/2011/04/congressional-freshmen-saddled-with.html, accessed August 1, 2011.

[3] http://www.opensecrets.org/politicians /summary.php?cid=N00000275& cycle=2010

[4] Interview, June 16, 2011.

[5] See Keith Poole and Howard Rosenthal's website, Voteview.com, for these data.

[6] I choose the 75% percentile because it seems a reasonable way to differentiate a minority of cases from the majority. The cut point was not chosen with an eye towards establishing the "best" fit possible.

[7] Nonlinear multilevel models fail to converge. Logistic regressions with fixed effects for state and year yield essentially the same results.

[8] In the model in which the dependent variable equals one when the candidate is in the 75th percentile or above in individual contributions, p=.004; in the model in which the dependent variable equals one when the candidate is in the 75th percentile or above in individual contributions below $200, p=.000.

6

What Survey Data Tells Us About Contributors

Chapter 5 focused on data available from the Federal Election Commission on campaign receipts. That data was well-suited for an examination of some – but not all – of the predictions on contribution patterns. In particular, predictions concerning the demand side of fundraising are easier to analyze with information whose source is the fundraisers themselves – that is, campaigns. Information on contributor motivations is more difficult to assess with such data, since we observe contributions only indirectly, through the receipts of the campaigns to which they contribute. We therefore must look elsewhere for further testing of the theories from Chapter 2.

For this purpose I turn to the National Election Studies, the most comprehensive survey dataset on American elections available to political scientists. Collected in some form since 1948, this dataset surveys between 1,000 and 2,500 individuals during each two year election cycle. Many other survey organizations also take polls every year, of course – some of them, such as Gallup, Pew, Rasmussen, and other professional polling outlets conduct surveys much more frequently. But many of these polls ask no more than one or two dozen questions, making it difficult to generate detailed analyses of what differentiates some respondents from others. A survey may ask whether voters approve of the president, for example, but may not collect information on their income and levels of education, or on whether they have voted for the same party in previous elections, or on their opinions about various policy issues. Without such questions, the typical commercial survey cannot tell us, for example, what proportion of supporters of gay marriage disapproves of President Obama. A more detailed survey allows us to tabulate this information, although there are always complications involving sampling error and other measurement problems.

In nearly every election cycle since 1952, the NES has asked respondents some variation on the question of whether they contributed money to a candidate or party. The minor differences in the question wording reflect the changing ways in which individuals engaged with politics over the course of the last century. In the 1950s and 1960s, for example, the survey asked respondents "Did you give any money or buy any tickets" to help a campaign or party. This reflects widespread use of event ticket sales as a fundraising device – not just tickets to the type of fundraising dinners we would recognize today, but also to golf days, boxing matches, picnics, and other entertainments organized by the campaigns or parties (see Heard 1960, Chapter 9). Since 1988, the NES has asked two straightforward questions: "Did you give money to an individual candidate running for public office?" and "Did you give money to a political party during this election year?"

Figure 6.1 shows the trend in contributing since 1952. The highest level recorded was in 1976, but the wording of the question in that year ("Did you give any money to a political party or make any other contribution this year") raises the possibility that some respondents believed they should answer in the affirmative if they had contributed to a non-political cause like a charity or church. Discarding the 1976 data point, the 13 percent of Americans who say they contributed to campaigns or parties in 2004 and 2008 represent an unprecedented figure – nearly doubling the proportion of Americans contributing in the mid-1990s.

The NES survey includes no specific questions about why respondents did or did not contribute money. It does, however, include a variety of questions about the emotional state of respondents, their engagement with politics, their degree of networked-ness, their willingness to discuss politics with family and friends, and other characteristics that will help us determine what distinguishes a contributor from a non-contributor.

In particular, the NES allows us to test key predictions developed in Chapter 2 regarding purposive incentives, expressive incentives generally, and the specific expressive incentives associated with socialization, as well as with emotion.

Figure 6.1: Percent of Respondents Reporting Having Contributed to a Candidate or Party, 1952-2008

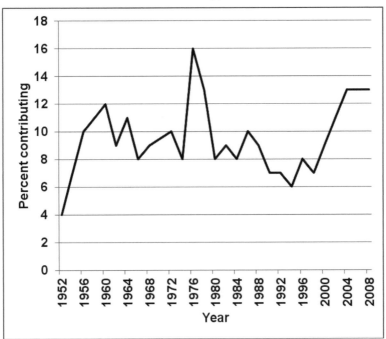

Source: American National Election Studies.

Purposive

Two key predictions of the purposive model are testable using the National Election Studies data.

People are more likely to contribute if they have strong preferences regarding goals.

This is the theory for which the NES provides the best and most comprehensive measures. Therefore, this is the theory that I test for most comprehensively in the data analysis that follows. There are two possible approaches to testing this theory. First, we could examine those people who have extreme views on an issue-by-issue basis. Those who are at extreme ends of the spectrum respecting, for example, abortion, the government's role in health care, and gay rights might be set apart from others, with the expectation that the more extreme would be more likely to contribute to a candidate or party than the less extreme.

The problem with this approach, however, is that we have no measures in the NES data of the relative salience of these issues to voters. Abortion may be the most important issue to a respondent, or it could be the least important issue to him or her. Without such a measure of salience relative to other issues on which these "extremists" might be moderates, it is unclear whether we would expect issue-by-issue extremists to contribute more often than others.

A second approach, and one that I use below, relies on general measures of extremism regarding attitudes towards the parties, partisanship, and liberalism/conservatism. Fortunately, the NES asks questions that allow for the construction of such measures.

I use three key variables to measure extremism, each of which has its advantages, but also has disadvantages. First, I use the NES "feeling thermometer" questions to construct a measure of extreme sentiment towards one or the other of the two major political parties. For the feeling thermometer questions, NES respondents are invited to rate organizations and individuals on a scale of zero to 100, with 100 representing very "warm" feelings and zero representing very "cold" feelings. For most politically-relevant groups and people, the mean ratings tend to be in the 55 to 65 range. To locate extremists, I generate a dichotomous variable coded one if a respondent rates one or the other major party either between zero and 5 or between 95 and 100. This divides the population into an "extremist" group representing 23 percent of respondents, and a "non-extremist" group of 77 percent of respondents.

A second measure of extremism considers partisanship directly. For decades, the NES has asked about respondents' party identification, first asking people to say whether they are a Democrat, a Republican, or what, and next asking whether the Democrats and Republicans consider themselves "strong" partisans, and whether those who identify as independents "lean: one way or the other. I create two dichotomous variables for "strong" Democrat" (19 percent of respondents) and "strong Republican" (11.4 percent). These strong partisans could be considered, for the purposes of the analysis that follows, "extreme."

Finally, I focus on ideology itself. The NES respondents are quizzed on whether they see themselves as liberal or conservative, and if so, whether they feel strongly or not so strongly about it. Measures of "strong liberal" and "strong conservative" result in too few cases in these categories (especially for liberals) to result in valid data analyses for several years in the survey. Accordingly, I broaden the scope of the ideological variable to encompass anyone who claims to be liberal or conservative. Liberals make up about 9 percent of the population; conservatives are 15 percent. Readers may find it surprising that so many Americans decline to commit to being one or the other, but studies of public opinion have long recognized that a large portion of the population does not see ideology as a particularly relevant category. The purposive theory would suggest that those who do not much care about ideology are unlikely to contribute to campaigns.

Each of these three measures of extremism has its drawbacks. Strong party identification could represent a commitment to the party programs, for example, but it could also indicate a merely social – not ideological – attachment. Those who identify as conservative may hold liberal views on some issues, or vice versa. Still, testing models that use all three of these measures rather than choosing to study just one of them ought to mitigate these deficiencies somewhat. If we see similar patterns when using all three of these variables to measure extremism, we can be quite confident of our conclusions with respect to the purposive model.

> People are more likely to contribute if they feel they can be influential in the accomplishment of a goal or sub-goal.

As discussed above in Chapter 2, purposive theory also predicts that individuals are likely to contribute if they see themselves as personally influential with respect to a particular goal or subgoal. Two good measures of one's perception of personal impact are their levels of internal and external efficacy. The first measure reflects a respondents' confidence that they can grasp the ins and outs of the political process, and the second measures the extent to which they feel as if they can personally impact the political system. The National Election Study questionnaire asks those surveyed whether they think politics is too complicated for them to understand, and also constructs an index based on questions about whether respondents believe government is responsive to people like them. I include both these measures in the analysis to come, to test people's perception of their own ability to impact the political system.

Expressive Incentives

Stemming from a somewhat different theoretical grounding than the theory of purposive incentives, the theory of expressive incentives focuses on the alleged personal benefits of contributing, regardless of the impact on campaigns, candidates, or public policy. There are two general predictions of the expressive incentives approach, as well as specific predictions associated with its social and emotional variants.

> People will contribute if the act of contributing provides an intrinsic benefit to them.

> People may contribute if they see contributions as intrinsically beneficial to them. The very act of contributing is itself the "consumption" of some kind of good. It is difficult in a survey to measure such intrinsic benefits, but the NES question on political interest probably comes as close as possible to such a measure. Those who are interested in politics may heighten their enjoyment (or their sense of entertainment) by becoming a first-hand participant in the political process, in the same way that those who purchase tickets to an NFL football game heighten their engagement by being present for the action, even though they could have watched the same event for free on television. I generate a political interest dummy variable, with 25 percent of the population qualifying as "interested."

> People's contributions should not depend on whether they feel (or possess) any causal agency towards the provision of a collective or public good.

This prediction of the expressive incentive approach is essentially the counter-hypotheses to the purposive prediction that those who feel as if they are likely to have an impact will contribute more often than those who feel that they have no impact. For the expressive incentive approach, it should not matter whether one has an impact, since the benefit of the contribution is linked to the contribution itself. Whether or not Obama or Ron Paul win the presidential race, their supporters will have benefited from their involvement. This hypothesis predicts that the internal and external efficacy variables described above will have little or no explanatory power.

Socially Defined Expressive Incentives

From whence does this intrinsic benefit of contributing come? There are at least two possibilities. The first is that they benefits of participation are socially defined.

> People are more likely to contribute the more socialized they are to respect common values associated with the political process and political goals.

One reason people may contribute is that they may be socialized to believe that contributing is a socially appropriate action, and that they are therefore better people for having contributed. Some models of voting, for example, have explained people's willingness to vote as reflection of what they believe to be their duty. If contributions work the same way, the "benefit" associated with contributing may simply be the sense that one has fulfilled one's duty – and the relief from the guilt feelings that one might experience if one shirked one's duty. The NES does not have a uniquely good measure of how well a person has been socialized to believe such things, but several variables allow us to zero in on the phenomenon. First, the NES asks whether it really matters if a person does not vote. Perhaps not surprisingly, the vast majority of Americans (nearly 84 percent) think it matters. (It is worth noting, however, how strongly this clashes with the rational choice theory of voting, which argues the reverse.) Unfortunately, the NES has asked this question only sporadically over time. Since 1980, it has only been asked in 2000 and 2002. Gauging its effect in these years alone will not give us a good sense of whether the effect of this variable is consistent, inconsistent, or changing over time.

Second, the NES asks respondents whether they discuss politics with their family and friends, an indicator of how central politics is to each respondent's daily life. Finally, the NES asks a standard question about one's level of education. Education levels have been associated with many factors that promote participation. In particular, those who are more educated possess the tools with which to surmount whatever structural barriers to participation may exist, such as voter registration requirements or polling places that are tough to find. For our purposes here, education might be seen as a proxy for political socialization, since many studies have found that higher education levels are associated with politically relevant variables such as tolerance, respect for the system, and a willingness to become involved.

Emotionally Defined Selective Incentives

> People who are affectively engaged with politics – particularly those whom politics makes more fearful – will be more likely to contribute.

Research on emotion and politics finds that those who are emotionally activated are at times more likely to take action – particularly if they are fearful. There is some evidence that the enthusiasm system may operate to drum up activity as well, but laboratory experiments tend to generate more consistent findings around fear. In each presidential election year since the 1970s, the NES has asked questions that allow for at least a rudimentary measure of emotional engagement. Each respondent is asked whether there is anything about each party's presidential candidate that made him or her "angry," "afraid," "hopeful," or "proud."

The extent to which these questions are really useful is debatable. Most experiments test the effects of immediate emotional reactions to something, rather than overarching sentiment, which is all a survey can measure, by design. Accordingly, if we see convincing evidence of a link between these affect questions and the propensity to contribute money, this would represent quite powerful evidence that affect has a key effect on contributions. If we see only marginal effects, it still may be the case that emotion has a connection to contributing, but that the data at hand are too unrefined to detect it.

Material and Solidary Incentives

Candidates can offer few or no material incentives for contributing to their campaigns. The contribution itself is costly, and campaigns are limited in the extent to which they can offer goods and services in exchange for contributions. Some campaigns sell buttons, bumper stickers, t-shirts or posters at a slight profit, but these are not a major source of individual contributions, nor would they necessarily appear in survey data about campaign contributions, since buyers of campaign paraphernalia might not see themselves as a contributor rather than a buyer or consumer.

The lack of clear material incentives for contributing is similar to candidates' constraints on offering rewards for voting, so it makes sense to examine the literature on voting for examples of how to handle material factors. There are few direct material incentives to voting, absent the presence of what party operatives used to call "walking around money" – essentially payoffs to organizers and voters for coming through for the party on election day. There are, however, a number of factors that researchers argue make voting less costly, such as higher education levels, income levels, and demographic characteristics such as age and church attendance that reflect a person's "embeddedness" in a community and therefore can serve as a proxy for the ease with which one can navigate the barriers to information gathering and voter registration requirements.

Working from the hypothesis that these factors may behave similarly when predicting contributions, I include variables for a person's age, income, gender, race, and education. Each of these factors may affect the costs that contributors perceive as going along with a contribution.

Church attendance and political discussion may also represent proxies for solidary incentives for participation, so each of these variables is subject to a dual interpretation. (See above for an interpretation of "political discussion" as a proxy for socially defined expressive incentives.) I also include a variable indicating whether a person was contacted by a campaign or party during the course of the campaign. Those who are contacted are usually those who are centrally located in social networks, so contact can represent significant social pressure for engagement (Rosenstone & Hansen 1993).

Analysis

My method of analysis is logistic regression, a statistical procedure that is appropriate when the dependent variable (the variable one is trying to explain, in this case, political contributions) takes on only two values. Here, individual respondents either contribute to political campaigns and parties, or they do not. Logistic regression allows us to estimate the effect each independent variable has on the probability that a person will contribute. Keep in mind that the overall probability of contributing is very low – only 7.8 percent of respondents in the entire dataset report having contributed; in 2008, the year with the most contributors since the 1970s, slightly more than 12 percent of people reported making a contribution. Slight shifts in the probability of contributing may therefore lead to significant changes in the numbers of people making donations. Because the overall probability of contributing is so low, I focus on how changes in key variables affect the probability of a contribution for a person who is already more likely than most people to make a contribution. This "reference person" is a middle-income, middle-aged, college educated, churchgoing female Democrat. In many logistic regression analyses, the analyst will report probability changes for "the typical case" in their dataset. Because the typical person in the NES is a non-contributor whose probability of contributing is unlikely to be large under any circumstances, I focus on people more likely to make a contribution. It is for these people that the marginal effects are likely to be larger.

Because the key effects are best understood in terms of probability changes, I report these probability changes in the main text and relegate detailed logistic regression outputs to the chapter appendices, where they can be consumed at will by the more statistically inclined. My analysis is restricted to the period between 1984 and 2008 due to the lack of availability of many key variables prior to 1984. As mentioned above, in earlier eras the question wording of "contribution" was different, so it is unclear whether analysis of data from the 1950s through the 1970s would be comparable in any case.

I first estimate models for presidential election years in the entire 1984 to 2008 period, reported in Table 6.1.

The first thing to note about the results is that several of the demographic characteristics that may make voting less costly – such as age and income – significantly increase the probability of making a contribution. A 59-year-old is over six percent more likely to contribute than a 32-year-old, holding all else equal. Raising a person's income from the second quintile to the fourth quintile has similar or slightly larger effects.

The key test for purposive incentives – whether ideological extremism increases the likelihood of contributing – provides clear confirmation of the purposive hypothesis. Depending on the measure of extremism being used, being an extremist raises the probability of contributing from between .033 and .111. Considering the fact that the baseline reference person has a probability of contributing of .102, increasing the probability by .111 more than doubles this person's chance of contributing.

It is also worth pointing out that the effects of extremism are stronger the more exclusive the group identified by the variable in question. Strong Democrats, who make up 19 percent of the population, are only .033 more likely to contribute, while strong Republicans, at 11 percent, are .111 more likely to contribute. Self-identified liberals, at only 9 percent of the population, are .10 more likely to give, while self-identified conservatives, at 15 percent, are only .034 more likely to contribute. Party identification alone appears to have only weak and inconsistent effects on contributing. Changing a voter from an independent to a (non-strong) Republican or Democrat has at best a .06 probability increase in the chance of contributing; at worst it has no significant effect at all. The narrower the ideological grouping, the more likely those who fall into that category are to participate in the campaign finance system.

Table 6.1: Effects on Predicted Probability of Contributing to a Campaign or Party – Presidential Years, 1984-2008

Baseline: Middle income 45-year-old white college educated, churchgoing female independent with strong political interest and efficacy, a habit of discussing politics, and contacted by a political party. Probability of contributing = .102

Measure of extremism	Effect on probability of contributing		
	"Extreme view of either political party"	"Liberal or conservative"	"Strong Democrat" and "strong Republican"
"Extreme view of either political party": 0 →1	.056***	--	--
Liberal: 0→1	--	.100***	--
Conservative 0→1	--	.034***	--
Strong Democrat: 0→1	--	--	.033***
Strong Republican 0→1	--	--	.111***
Income: 2nd quintile → 4th quintile	.074***	.068***	.068***
Not interested→ interested	.053***	.049***	.049***
"Discuss politics with family and friends": 0 → 1	.038***	.034***	.034***
Age: 32 (25th percentile) → 59 (75th percentile)	.066***	.066***	.061***
Sex: female → male	.006	.005	.007
Race: white → black	-.031**	-.019	-.028**
Race: white → Hispanic	.014	-.008	-.012
Party ID: independent → Democrat	.055**	.039*	.036*
Party ID: independent → Republican	.060***	.050**	.019
Education: no college → college	.051***	.042***	.047***

Church: non-attender → attender	-.003	-.001	-.005
Efficacy: low → high	.032***	.028***	.026***
Contact: not contacted →contacted	.055***	.050***	.051***
Democratic pres. candidate made angry	.035***	.031***	.032***
Democratic pres. candidate made afraid	.009	.009	.008
Democratic pres. candidate made hopeful	-.011	-.011	-.008
Democratic pres. candidate made proud	.048***	.044***	.047***
Republican pres. candidate made angry	.022**	.016***	.022**
Republican pres. candidate made afraid	.033***	.028***	.035***
Republican pres. candidate made hopeful	-.006	-.007	-.010
Republican pres. candidate made proud	.009	.010	.005

*p<.10; **p<.05;***p<.01

The efficacy variable – measuring how much of an impact a person feels he or she can have on the political process, has significant but smaller effects on the likelihood that a person will donate to campaigns or parties. At most, high efficacy people are .032 more likely to contribute – an increase in the chances of contributing roughly half that of age.

Small as it may be, the presence of a significant effect of efficacy on contributing does not support one of the key elements of expressive giving – that contributors care little or not at all about the impact of their contributions. Another prediction of the expressive theory, that people will contribute if the act of contributing provides an intrinsic benefit to them, gets stronger support from the model. Those who say they are interested in politics increase their probability of giving by about .05.

While not as strong as that of ideological extremism, this effect is significant and consistent across all three models.

Those who are embedded in social networks (discussing politics with their family and friends) and those whose background may have socialized them to participate more in politics (those with higher levels of education) are also significantly more likely to contribute, although these effects are generally smaller than the effects of political interest and ideological extremism. This provides mild evidence in support of the socially-defined expressive incentive hypotheses. Interestingly, however, church attendance appears to have no effect on contributing. It may be that those who are high church attenders are not more likely to contribute to politics because any tendency to contribute more to a cause may be directed at the religious groups to which the respondent belongs.

The variables measuring various emotional categories have mixed effects on contributing. Anger at one or the other presidential candidate seems to be associated with higher levels of contributing (with effects comparable to efficacy or political discussion), but the fear variable does not have consistent effects – those who fear the Republican are more likely to contribute, but greater fear about the Democratic presidential candidate do not contribute any more than others. On the other hand, pride in the Democratic candidate elicits contributions, while pride in the Republican candidate does not. Emotion does seem to play a role in contributing, but its effects would appear to differ by party, and would appear to be more complex than the simple theories outlined above would suggest. It may be that survey questions asked of respondents days, weeks, or months after a contribution are incapable of measuring precisely the emotional context within which a contribution was made.

Effects of Extremism over Time

Of the key theoretical predictions about intangible incentives for giving, the hypothesis about ideological extremism appears to have the strongest support. This finding provides the supply-side counterpart of the finding in Chapter 5 that incumbent candidates who are more ideologically extreme collect a larger proportion of their funds from small individual contributors. A useful next step is to examine how the effect of extremism on giving has changed over time.

To examine the effects of extremism over the years, I re-estimate separate logistic regression models for each election year from 1984 to 2008 (except 2006, in which the NES did not conduct a standard time series study). I report the detailed results of all these models in the Appendices. In Figure 6.2, I plot the predicted effects of extremism over

Figure 6.2: Predicted Effects of Extremism on Probability of Contributing, 1984-2008

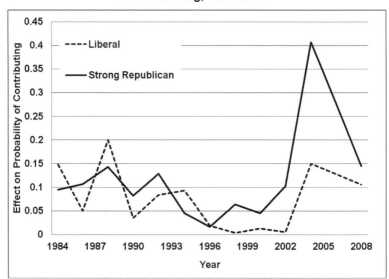

time, using the categories of extremism that are the narrowest, and that have the largest effects in the full models reported above: "liberal" and "strong Republican."

As the figure shows, extreme political views had clear effects in the 1980s, but declined in their impact through the decade of the 1990s. Beginning around 2000, however, the effect of extreme views surged, to the point where in 2004, strong Republicans had a .40 higher probability of contributing than did others. For liberals, the probability of contributing went up as well, reaching at least the levels of the 1980s.

Clearly one possibility is that the rise of the internet is in some way responsible for this effect. It may be that the ease of contributing online provides particular encouragement for the ideologically committed, making it more likely that they will contribute, while having little effect on others. To test for such an effect, I generated an interaction term that combined the liberal and strong Republican variables with a variable indicating whether or not a respondent had access to the internet. For the years 2004 and 2008, this interaction term is positive and significant for liberals, consistent with the hypothesis that the internet is responsible for the recent rise in the effect of extremism on contributing. For strong Republicans, however, the interaction term has no effect. Perhaps the left has relied more on the internet than the right in recent campaigns, leaving conservatives to mobilize through talk radio, outlets such as FOX News, and other means. Some research on the Tea Party movement suggests that FOX plays a key organizing role for passionate conservatives (Williamson, Skocpol, & Coggin 2011). The diverse effects of new technology and new media on contribution patterns would seem to offer fertile ground for future research.

Figure 6.2 also adds evidence to Chapter 5's discovery that the effect of candidate extremism on the collection of individual contributions has changed in the most recent election cycles. Although we do not have NES data for 2010, the predicted effect of individual-level extremism on the probability that a person will make a political donation remains high in the 2008 model. Aside from 2004, the predicted effect in 2008 is the highest in two decades. This adds further evidence in favor of the hypothesis that the effect of candidate extremism remains high, but has become non-linear in recent years. Prospective contributors may be seeking out those candidates who have uniformly extreme positions, rather than considering contributions to more moderate candidates. This data analysis does not provide a direct test of this hypothesis, however.

Conclusion

Public opinion surveys taken over the last three decades confirm that intangible incentives play a key role in campaign contribution patterns. Those who are more interested in politics, feel that their voices will be heard, and are embedded in social networks that reinforce the values of political involvement and good citizenship are more likely than others to contribute to campaigns and causes. Each of these factors, however, is eclipsed in importance by the effect of having political views that place a respondent in a small minority on one or the other side of the ideological spectrum. The effects of ideology ebbed in the 1990s, but resurged with a vengeance in the last decade, perhaps due to the effects of the internet and other new media and technology.

In 1978, the Nobel Prize-winning economist Douglass North mused about what accounted for the 19th century farm protest movements in the United States, in which countless small farmers fought government policies and railroad barons at great cost to their own careers and in some cases to their personal safety. He concluded that what prompted so many small farmers to "raise less corn and more hell" in defiance of the logic of collective action was their great sense of the injustice that had been done to them. "It may be irrational for farmers to ignore the free rider problem in organizing to transfer the gains of lower transportation costs to themselves," wrote North, "but they did so because of fundamental convictions about the injustice of the distribution of income" (North 1978, p. 974).

Individual contributors to political campaigns do not, on the whole, face injustices comparable to those of the farmers who joined the protest movements of the 19th century. But neither do they make sacrifices that are nearly so great. For both groups, however, ideological conviction appears to surmount clear collective action problems. As previous research on political participation has shown, age, income, political interest, and embeddedness in social networks all affect the likelihood of making contributions. But ideological passion also generates contributions, and has done so increasingly in recent years.

Table 6.2: Logistic Regression Models Predicting Political Donations, 1984-2008;
Measure of Extremism: 95 or above or 5 or below on at least one party feeling thermometer

	1984	1986	1988	1990	1992	1994	1996	1998	2000	2004	2008
Extremism											
Party feeling thermometers	.56**	.14	.36	.21	.05	.61**	.26	.40	.94***	.74***	.43*
Engagement											
Democrat	.15	.33	.64	1.60**	.28	1.11	1.52*	.64	.38	.86	.71
Republican	.36	.41	.71	1.36*	-0.13	1.51*	1.91**	.69	.58	.85	.56
Political interest	1.15***	1.10***	.65***	.67***	1.02***	.81***	.29	.84***	.68**	1.07***	.61**
Internal efficacy	.38*	--	--	.43*	.15	-0.02	-0.15	.48*	.08	--	.91***
External efficacy	.51**	-0.30	.64***	.92***	.28	.06	.08	-0.03	.30	.29	.52*
Discuss politics	1.16***	1.13***	--	.36	1.44***	.68	1.20***	1.05*	.96***	1.14***	-0.01
Contacted	1.06***	.64***	.68***	.91***	.74***	.94***	.71***	.49*	.82***	.59**	1.03***
Church attendance	-0.82***	-0.02	.04	.05	.04	.35	.19	-0.12	-.34	-0.00	.19
Affect											
Angry (Dem)	.32	--	--	--	.46**	--	.15	--	.02	.60**	.20
Afraid (Dem)	-0.10	--	--	--	.14	--	.23	--	.43	.37	-0.11
Hopeful (Dem)	.23	--	--	--	-0.16	--	-0.10	--	-0.01	.55*	-0.60**
Proud (Dem)	.39*	--	--	--	.19	--	.29	--	.33	.10	.83***
Angry (Rep)	-0.15	--	--	--	-0.02	--	.39	--	.19	-.42	.61***
Afraid (Rep)	.14	--	--	--	.19	--	.15	--	.19	-.55*	.92***
Hopeful (Rep)	.04	--	--	--	-0.04	--	-0.57**	--	.39	-.30	-0.12
Proud (Rep)	-0.41	--	--	--	.23	--	.59*	--	.21	-.28	.23
Demographics											
Age	.02***	.02***	.04***	.03***	.03***	.03***	.04***	.04**	.03***	.04***	.02***
Female	.09	.24	.04	.32	-0.15	-0.19	-0.37*	.15	-0.04	.25	-0.01
Black	-0.40	-0.23	.35	-.32	-1.04**	.35	-.18	-0.78	-0.09	-0.24	-0.27
Hispanic	.01	-0.44	-.42	.09	-0.00	-0.48	.55	.44	.53	-0.66	-0.69**
College education	.94***	.44**	1.22***	.65***	.45**	.43	.84***	.62*	.26	.85***	.82***
Income(2q)	1.15*	-0.38	.94	-0.23	.19	.48	-0.12	-1.04	1.87***	-0.95*	-0.32
Income(3q)	1.71***	.70*	1.41***	.06	.54	1.14**	.37	-0.27	1.99***	-0.11	.12
Income(4q)	1.96***	1.55***	2.23***	.70*	.75*	1.45*	.97*	.47	2.72***	.16	.60
Income(5q)	2.52***	1.67***	3.15***	1.78***	1.81***	3.28***	1.86***	.92*	2.78***	.72	1.43***
Constant	-8.36***	-6.39***	-8.19***	-7.44***	-7.21***	-8.64***	-9.33***	-7.23***	-9.26***	-7.00***	-6.38***
N	1,982	1,984	1,862	1,792	2,281	1,649	1,563	1,205	1,512	1,070	2,115

*p<.10 **p<.05 ***p<.01

Table 6.3: Logistic Regression Models Predicting Political Donations, 1984-2008;
Measure of extremism: Self-identified liberal or conservative

	1984	1986	1988	1990	1992	1994	1996	1998	2000	2002	2004	2008
Extremism												
Liberal	.79***	.31	1.17***	.38	.51*	1.18***	.94***	.05	.21	.06	.82**	.82***
Conservative	-0.07	.19	.86***	.50*	.16	.02	.65**	-0.12	-0.73*	.43*	.98***	.73***
Engagement												
Democrat	.13	.32	.51	1.59**	.18	.91	1.35*	.63	.45	.65	.85	.55
Republican	.42	.39	.50	1.31*	-0.18	1.64**	1.74**	.71	.71	.90*	.63	.35
Political interest	1.12***	1.07***	.56**	.65***	1.01***	.77***	.24	.89***	.80***	.87***	1.02***	.62**
Internal efficacy	.30	--	--	.36	.13	.02	-0.19	.51*	.02	--	--	.84***
External efficacy	.55**	-.029	.61***	.94***	.28	-0.02	-0.01	-0.03	.26	.21	.23	.48
Discuss politics	1.18***	1.12***	--	.32	1.43***	.63	1.11**	1.04*	.95**	.90**	1.21***	.02
Contacted	1.04***	.65***	.67***	.89***	.73***	.97***	.68***	.48*	.84***	.76***	.53**	1.00***
Church attendance	-0.76***	-0.03	.04	.03	.06	.46*	.16	-0.09	-0.37	.01	-0.02	.12
Affect												
Angry (Dem)	.30	--	--	--	.45**	--	.11	--	.07	--	.56**	.22
Afraid (Dem)	-0.04	--	--	--	.12	--	.11	--	.46	--	.33	-0.07
Hopeful (Dem)	.21	--	--	--	-0.16	--	-0.06	--	-0.13	--	.64**	-0.54*
Proud (Dem)	.43*	--	--	--	.19	--	.28	--	.40	--	.02	.82***
Angry (Rep)	-0.18	--	--	--	-0.05	--	.36	--	.20	--	-0.58*	.56**
Afraid (Rep)	.05	--	--	--	.18	--	.08	--	.21	--	-0.42	.91***
Hopeful (Rep)	.05	--	--	--	-0.06	--	-0.54*	--	.25	--	-0.25	-0.18
Proud (Rep)	-0.40	--	--	--	.30	--	.59*	--	.27	--	-0.36	.24
Demographics												
Age	.02***	.02***	.04***	.03***	.03***	.04***	.05***	.04***	.04***	.03***	.04***	.03***
Female	.09	.26	.16	.34	-0.15	-0.16	-0.40*	.19	-0.00	-0.81***	.25	-0.06
Black	-0.28	-0.20	.39	-0.29	-0.99**	.47	-0.08	-0.67	-0.01	.12	-0.07	-0.08
Hispanic	.12	-0.39	-0.28	.15	.04	-0.44	.60	.49	.55	.23	-0.54	-0.64**
College education	.86***	.42*	1.21***	.60**	.40*	.29	.74**	.57*	.10	.30	.72**	.63***
Income (2q)	1.14	-0.42	.97*	-0.26	.17	.35	-0.15	-1.04	1.73**	--	-0.97*	-0.39
Income(3q)	1.71**	.68*	1.44***	.02	.53	1.06*	.37	-0.31	1.80***	--	-0.22	.09
Income(4q)	1.90***	1.51***	2.20***	.69*	.75*	1.36**	.96*	.46	2.51***	--	.11	.52
Income(5q)	2.46***	1.66***	3.08***	1.83***	1.82***	3.18***	1.81***	.88*	2.58***	--	.61	1.37***
Constant	-8.36***	-6.38***	-8.44***	-7.42***	-7.23***	-8.53***	-9.25	-7.20***	-8.78***	-5.99***	-7.05***	-6.30***
N	1,982	1,984	1,862	1,792	2,281	1,649	1,563	1,205	1,512	1,500	1,070	2,115

*p<.10 **p<.05 ***p<.01

Table 6.4: Logistic Regression Models Predicting Political Donations, 1984-2008; Measure of extremism: Self-identified "strong Democrat" or "strong Republican"

	1984	1986	1988	1990	1992	1994	1996	1998	2000	2002	2004	2008
Extremism												
Strong Democrat	.12	.77***	.14	.39	.37	.51	.63*	.88**	-0.16	.79**	.09	.51*
Strong Republican	.52*	.61**	.88***	.75**	.76***	.74**	.81***	.81**	.69**	.94***	1.82***	1.00***
Engagement												
Democrat	.14	.03	.61	1.44*	.13	.96	1.28	.26	.46	.32	.80	.46
Republican	.21	.17	.32	1.08	-0.44	1.23	1.65**	.29	.40	.64	.11	.17
Political interest	1.17***	1.02***	.58***	.61***	.95***	.74***	.20	.76	.75***	.80***	1.11***	.55*
Internal efficacy	.35*	--	--	.43*	.15	-0.04	-0.17	.50*	.03	--	--	.93***
External efficacy	.46**	-0.34*	.59***	.87***	.22	-0.03	.02	-0.06	.21	.15	.24	.44
Discuss politics	1.11***	1.09***	--	.33	1.49***	.59	1.17***	.95	.94**	.92**	1.08**	-0.01
Contacted	1.04***	.64***	.70***	.87***	.73***	.95***	.75***	.34	.85***	.80***	.59**	1.01***
Church attendance	-0.79***	-0.06	.00	-0.01	.01	.30	.12	-0.10	-0.40	-0.04	-0.09	.12
Affect												
Angry (Dem)	.30	--	--	--	.43*	--	.17	--	.05	--	.56**	.21
Afraid (Dem)	-0.05	--	--	--	.11	--	.20	--	.40	--	.21	-0.08
Hopeful (Dem)	.24	--	--	--	-0.11	--	-0.08	--	.00	--	.75**	-0.58**
Proud (Dem)	.45**	--	--	--	.13	--	.31	--	.43	--	.04	.88***
Angry (Rep)	-0.13	--	--	--	-0.02	--	.36	--	.24	--	-0.36	.61***
Afraid (Rep)	.12	--	--	--	.22	--	.11	--	.23	--	-0.46	.95***
Hopeful (Rep)	-0.02	--	--	--	-0.07	--	-0.62**	--	.27	--	-0.45	-0.18
Proud (Rep)	-0.43	--	--	--	.28	--	.52*	--	.17	--	-0.30	.18
Demographics												
Age	.02***	.02***	.04***	.03***	.03***	.03***	.04***	.04***	.04***	.03***	.04***	.02***
Female	.09	.23	.00	.32	-0.15	-0.18	-0.42*	.15	.04	-0.86***	.13	-0.06
Black	-0.31	-0.37	.39	-0.33	-1.09**	.37	-0.23	-0.94	.04	-0.12	-0.15	-0.33
Hispanic	.08	-0.51	-0.37	.11	-0.01	-0.46	.59	.43	.61	.36	-0.61	-0.74**
College education	.93***	.48***	1.20***	.66***	.46**	.36	.82***	.62*	.11	.35	.82***	.80***
Income (2q)	1.11	-0.39	.90	-0.24	.22	.41	-0.08	-1.07	1.74**	--	-1.11**	-0.38
Income(3q)	1.68**	.70*	1.35***	.06	.57	1.14**	.35	-0.23	1.75***	--	-0.25	.00
Income(4q)	1.90***	1.56***	2.16***	.72*	.82*	1.46**	1.01*	.57	2.49***	--	-0.03	.49
Income(5q)	2.43***	1.67***	3.10***	1.77***	1.87***	3.31***	1.79***	.87*	2.53***	--	.52	1.28***
Constant	-8.12***	-6.25***	-8.02***	-7.27***	-7.23***	-8.41***	-9.19***	-6.96***	-8.79***	-5.87***	-6.67***	-6.08***
N	1,982	1,984	1,862	1,792	2,281	1,649	1,563	1,205	1,512	1,500	1,070	2,115

*p<.10 **p<.05 ***p<.01

7
Why Do People Give?

During the 2008 presidential campaign, I heard the following story from a friend. Her father, a liberal academic who lives in Illinois, would spend more time than might have been strictly healthy watching vitriolic opinion shows on one of the major news networks. Every so often, after a politician or talking head said something especially offensive to his political sensibilities, this man would leap up and exclaim, "Argh! I've got to give more money to Barack Obama." Off to the computer he would go, credit card in hand.

The previous chapters have tested a series of explanations of why people contribute to political campaigns and causes. In Chapter 5, I focused on what aggregate data available from the Federal Election Commission can tell us about giving patterns, and found that purposive motives appear to explain a significant portion of individual giving patterns – particularly among those who contribute small amounts to campaigns.

In Chapter 6 I focused on individual level data, using the National Election Studies surveys to examine more individual-level motives, including material incentives, solidary incentives, purposive incentives, emotionally-defined expressive incentives, and socially defined expressive incentives. That data analysis, too, suggested that purposive motives, and perhaps to a lesser extent expressive motives, can explain variation that is not explained by more traditional material and social factors.

These data are necessarily incomplete. They reflect what candidates report to the Federal Election Commission and what individuals tell survey researchers in short conversations. But they seem consistent with my friend's father's 2008 giving patterns. Passionate feelings prompted him to access the computer and make a donation in a situation in which other people might have stayed seated on the couch, perhaps switching the channel to sports or entertainment programming.

Based on the analysis above, coupled with information from interviews with political professionals and previous research on the subject, we can identify three main categories of contributors: solidary givers, material givers, and purposive givers. Expressive givers as defined in Chapter 2 may exist, but the evidence in their favor is shakier – especially as respects emotionally-defined expressive incentives. Candidates, campaign managers and finance directors build their funder coalitions by assessing their appeal to all three main types of contributor.

Each campaign may be treated as if it decides on a sum that is necessary to raise, and then seeks to generate funders from various sources in order to reach that goal. (In fact, the fundraising goal may change during the campaign due to unforeseen competition or other factors, but this complication merely changes the targets; it does not fundamentally change the process.) Almost all campaigns begin with the solidary givers. These are the candidate's friends, family, former classmates, and others in what political scientist Richard Fenno would call the personal constituency (Fenno 1978).

After the initial appeal to the personal constituency, candidates emphasize different fundraising techniques depending on the resources available to them. This effort is essentially an exercise in solving a collective action problem. Solutions to such problems often depend on the strategies of the organizers, as well as – crucially – the resources the organizers have at their disposal.

Candidates for Congress have two general sorts of resources. First, they may offer some kind of material benefit that depends on their access to the policy-making process. This material exchange has not been the focus of this book, but other authors have conceived of it as involving favors, access, effort, or other kinds of policy-related goods. Scholars have searched with mixed success for evidence of quid-pro-quo exchanges because in a situation in which someone is organizing for collective action, you would not expect a quid-pro-quo that involved a change in the organizer's attitude. Interest group leaders do not often change their minds in response to their contributors' wishes; they seek out contributors who agree with them and attempt to goad them into contributing to the common goal. As with interest group organizers, the material benefit that candidates offer their contributors is likely to be more like a "side payment" related to, but not the same as, the goal of "good policy" that both the contributor and the candidate hold in common.

Second, the candidate can make an individual's contribution intangibly more satisfying. Interest group scholars have developed a variety of specifications for the possible intangible rewards that are available for contributing, discussed above in Chapter 2. Although it is possible that other kinds of intangible rewards (particularly emotional rewards) are also effective, evidence from candidate financial reports and public opinion surveys suggest that purposive rewards are a significant motivator. Candidates can offer more effective purposive rewards if they have clear, distinct, and ideologically pleasing positions. Moderates and equivocators need not apply. Just as a sharp ideological appeal will prompt applause in a debate setting, such an appeal is likely to elicit individual contributions of $5, $10, or $25.

Of course, not everyone attends a debate, much less applauds at one, and not everyone ponies up a contribution to a political campaign. On the contrary, even though the U.S. has seen a recent surge in individual contributions, no more than 13 percent of people actually give – a figure somewhere between the percent of Americans who say they regularly watch MSNBC and the percent who say they regularly watch FOX News in the fall of an election year.[1] Not every American who has an extreme view about an issue is a sure bet to donate. Just as the National Rifle Association does not collect dues from every gun owner and the AARP does not enroll every retired person, candidates cannot expect to succeed in extracting money from every politically passionate individual who shares their view of the world.

Predicting who will give for purposive reasons and who will not is an uncertain task, and it is therefore understandable that some campaigns choose not to focus on this source of contributions. As Clark and Wilson argued in 1961, those who rely on purposive incentives are on less sure footing than those who rely on other inducements. The candidates who do not seek out such contributors are usually the ones that can easily offer other selective incentives to other kinds of contributors. They may be incumbents with a plumb committee assignment that makes PAC solicitation easier. They may be socially well connected to a relatively wealthy network of friends and family. Those campaigns that do not have these advantages – such as that of Mark Neumann in Wisconsin – can find that it pays off to focus on small donors. Even among incumbents, Chapter 5 showed that those candidates who have extreme views on one side or the other of the political spectrum collect more of their money in smaller amounts.

Individuals give to politics for a variety of tangible and intangible reasons. As many studies of participation have shown, those who do contribute tend to be wealthier, older, and better connected than those who do not. Knowing that passionate people are also more likely to contribute can be as important a fact for campaigns as knowing that people who join many groups are more likely to give, or that people who discuss politics with others are likely to be more motivated to donate. Each piece of information provides campaigns with knowledge about a resource that it can make use of in designing a fundraising strategy.

Individuals usually do not give to campaigns unprompted, just as interest group members do not join if they have not been contacted by the organization in some way. When campaigns decide who to contact, though, they consider individual characteristics such as income, age, networks, and passion. Public opinion data suggest that this last category may be becoming even more important in the 21st century than it has been in the past.

---

[1] "Americans Spend More Time Following the News," Pew Research Center for the People and the Press, September 12, 2010, http://www.people-press.org/2010/09/12/section-1-watching-reading-and-listening-to-the-news/, accessed December 16, 2011.

8

Whither the Campaign Finance System?

The previous chapters have focused on the important but relatively narrow question of why individuals contribute to candidates and political causes. This was an important question to ask because most previous political science research on campaign finance assumed that the answer was self-evident: that they wanted some material benefit from a politician or the political process as a whole. This turned out to be part of the answer, although it was not nearly the whole story. Instead, people give for a variety of reasons, grouped together by Verba, Schlozman, and Brady in the general categories of resources, networks, and desire or taste for participation (Verba, Schlozman, & Brady 1995). I have argued that taste for participation can be thought of as a purposive or expressive incentive, and that purposive incentives in particular are an important part of the explanation for campaign fundraising patterns over the past thirty years.

In this chapter, I broaden the focus to discuss the campaign finance system as a whole. One point that reformers have made for decades – if not centuries – is that those who finance campaigns have some influence on how politics is conducted and on how policy gets made. The system should therefore be reformed, these critics argue, to shut out certain sources of campaign money. What have our discoveries about individual contributor motivations and campaign fundraising coalitions taught us about how modern contributors may be shaping the system?

Campaigns as Interest Groups

The job of a candidate is not too different from the job of an interest group organizer. Just as the interest group organizer must solve the problem of how to form and manage a group, so must the candidate solve the problem of how to launch and maintain an effective campaign organization. These problems are different in nature from those facing a private entrepreneur, since the private entrepreneur deals in private goods – goods that can be bought and sold. Candidates and interest group organizers deal in collective goods. Each interest group focuses on a policy goal or goals that affect broad populations roughly equally. Similarly, candidates favor goals of "good policy" that their supporters presumably share (Fenno 1978).

Collective goods invite free rider problems. Individuals – even if they approve of the collective good in principle – will find it irrational to contribute, knowing that their contributions are unlikely to be decisive and reasoning that they will benefit from the collective good in any case, if it is indeed provided. To surmount the barrier that the collective action problem represents, campaigns and interest groups alike must resort to selective incentives.

Far from being mechanistic, however, solving collective action problems can be a dynamic process. Interest group organizers and candidates operate in a world in which many strategies and choices are possible. This insight has been fruitful for the research on interest groups. Witness Terry Moe's description of the political entrepreneur who seeks to organize a group and thus maximize his "surplus" (that is to say, his personal benefit):

> ...[T]here are alternative strategies available to him. There are many ways to organize a group and many ways thereby to derive a surplus, leaving the entrepreneur with a range of possible actions from which to choose. Most obviously, he might choose to emphasize either collective goods or selective incentives, or perhaps both. Which he chooses to stress will determine the kinds of individuals that respond, the contributions forthcoming, the actions required, and so on, all of which bear directly upon his own surplus, the survival prospects of the group, and the manner in which the organization must be structured (Moe 1980, p. 38).

Candidates do the same thing. In building their fundraising coalitions, they consider their areas of comparative advantages in fundraising, and they focus disproportionately on these areas, as the data analysis in Chapter 5 shows. Those who raise most of their money from small individual contributions tend to focus more on purposive incentives than those who raise most of their money from PACs.

The parallel between candidates and interest groups suggests a number of implications for campaigns based on the past few decades of interest group research. Since the 1960s, groups have become more numerous, more professionalized, more centralized, and more elite-focused (Skocpol 2003). Technological change as well as new models of lobbying and electioneering have led groups to focus their appeals more narrowly on those most likely to support them, targeting precisely those people who are most likely to respond with a contribution (Heclo 2000, Schier 2000). The result is that groups that represent the interests of relatively wealthy and relatively passionate people have flourished, while groups that represent the interests of the less well off and the less passionate have diminished in their influence and, in some cases, perished.

Something similar appears to have happened in congressional campaigns. The technological innovations and victory strategies that interest groups have adopted are in many cases useful for running for office. Candidates may have experience in interest group organizing, as did Barack Obama, or they may benefit from those who have experience in the private sector, as did Ron Paul. Many of the businesses that aid campaigns in fundraising also aid interest groups. Ideas, technologies, and skills cannot help but cross-pollinate. It should therefore be no surprise that political scientist Larry Bartels, for example, finds that Senators tend to represent the interests of their wealthy constituents more effectively than they represent the interests of the poor (Bartels 2008).

The Future of Campaign Finance

What does this mean for the world of campaign finance?

The result of the way the current campaign finance system is structured is that incumbent members of Congress rarely face competition, and even more rarely face competition from a candidate representing the interests of the non-wealthy and non-passionate. I begin this section by reviewing some previously suggested campaign reforms that I think have little chance of improving the situation. I conclude with some suggestions of my own.

Very Low Contribution Limits

Some reformers suggest that PAC contributions be banned and that contributions from individuals be limited to a very low level such as $100 or $200. This impulse was behind the 2008 Obama campaign's claims that their small-donor base amounted to a "parallel public finance system." Advocates of this or similar measures argue that interested money would be largely driven out of the system in favor of disinterested contributions from millions of ordinary Americans.

The problem with this idea is that ordinary Americans do not contribute money to campaigns. As the data analysis in Chapters 5 and 6 shows, small contributions are not interested money in the same way that PAC contributions usually are, but they represent interested money nevertheless. Contributors are more extreme and more passionate about politics, not to mention wealthier and more engaged in social networks than most. Cutting out PAC money and forcing campaigns to focus their fundraising energies on this group of contributors would give clear advantages to those candidates with more extreme views, and would thus aggravate the existing problems associated with congressional polarization. Outside ideological groups with the power to mobilize millions of small contributors, such as the liberal MoveOn.org or the conservative Americans for Tax Reform would become more important in such a system.

Spending Limits

Since the Supreme Court's 1976 *Buckley* v. *Valeo* ruling, mandatory spending limits have been unconstitutional. Today's spending limit proposals involve "voluntary" limits, with participating candidates rewarded with a sizeable infusion of public financing (about which more later).

Spending limits by themselves do little to address the underlying collective action problem facing many potential campaigns, however. To see why, imagine that there was a cap on how much interest groups could spend on organization and lobbying. In such a world, the interest group world would probably not look very different from the way it looks today; certain groups would spend less, but there would not be a sudden surge in new groups representing the previously underrepresented. Similarly, under a spending limits regime, some candidates would spend somewhat less, but the overall distribution of types of candidates would remain the same.

In fact, as some political scientists have pointed out, spending limits may harm challengers because the marginal benefit per dollar spent is higher for them than it is for incumbents (Jacobson 1978, 1990; Gerber 2004). Depending on the level at which they are set, therefore, spending limits could cut challengers off before they have a chance to be competitive.

Public Financing

Public financing, the distribution of government funds to candidates for use on campaign activities, has some promise in solving collective action problems in a way that might make campaigns more competitive. The problem concerns the way most of the public financing proposals are structured. In many cases, funds are distributed to candidates who demonstrate their 'viability' by raising a significant number of small contributions in amounts ranging from $5 to $250. After qualifying for funds, candidates may then receive public funds to match further small contributions. This structure has the effect of replicating the problem with a system of very low contribution limits. Candidates will succeed if they can appeal to the very passionate small donor base, and moderate candidates who may be more representative of the median voter may be disadvantaged.

In addition to this difficulty, public financing proposals tend to go hand-in-hand with spending limits, a policy of which I am skeptical for the reasons stated above. If a public financing scheme were to successfully address the collective action problem inherent in funding a campaign organization, it should cast a very wide net for eligible candidates, should distribute sizeable amounts of public funds in lump-sum payments, and should not be associated with spending limits. I cannot envision such a plan winning the support it would need to be enacted by a legislature or the U.S. Congress.

Similar problems would seem to plague proposals such as the "patriot dollars" plan advocated by Bruce Ackerman and Ian Ayres (Ackerman & Ayres 2004). They propose offering all Americans a credit card with which they could direct a $50 contribution to the candidate of their choice. Although these contributions would essentially be free, it is hard to believe that they would not disproportionately be given by those who felt passionately enough to bother to donate. Ackerman and Ayres would make the identity of contributors anonymous, but this would do nothing to counter the power of ideological groups that could direct the flow of donations simply by pointing out to partisans the candidates that meet particular ideological litmus tests.

Solving Collective Action Problems

"The flaw in the pluralist heaven," wrote E.E. Schattschneider in 1960, "is that the heavenly chorus sings with a distinct upper class accent" (Schattschneider 1960, p. 35). Since 1960, the accented chorus has grown louder in the world of interest groups and has pervaded the world of political campaigns as well. When Schattschneider wrote of this problem more than five decades ago, he recommended expanding the scope of conflict, drawing new participants in so as to make the debate more representative of the average American.

Another way to put this is that collective action ought to be subsidized for the people who find it difficult or impossible to organize for collective action today. Candidates for office build their fundraising coalitions today by appealing to those who are easy to organize – those who have incentives to participate for material, social, or purposive reasons. A coalition built from this set of building blocks will almost certainly be unrepresentative. If candidates who cannot appeal to these sources are to be competitive, either their natural allies ought to be subsidized, or the candidates themselves should be subsidized.

I am skeptical of efforts to subsidize potential individual donors directly, for the reasons outlined above. Those of us who find politics fascinating may have a hard time admitting it, but most Americans consider political campaigns to be annoying or boring or both. I doubt that new subsidies for engagement would change this very much, leading us back to where we started with funding coalitions that are unrepresentative, elite, and extreme.

A better bet is to subsidize institutions that have incentives to improve competitiveness. Rick Hall suggests the creation of an "expenditure equalizing committee," a non-profit endowment-funded agency that would contribute funds to underfunded candidates (Hall 2007). A similar idea would be to set up a tax status that allowed PACs to collect money far in excess of federally-set limits, but only if they contribute this money to campaigns that were behind their opponents in the most recent FEC filing. In each case, an institution or set of institutions would have incentives to seek out underfunded but viable candidates and help solve their collective action problems. Elections would be more competitive and more people would be represented.

The main difficulty with these proposals is that they may not survive constitutional scrutiny. The 2008 Supreme Court ruling in *Davis* v. *FEC* struck down a law that imposed different contribution limits on different types of candidates (the specific law at issue was the so-called "millionaire's provision" of the 2002 campaign reform act that lifted contribution limits for candidates facing self-financed opponents). The Court's logic that such laws "impermissibly burden" the speech of particular candidates and create a "drag on First Amendment rights" would seem to apply to the "equalizing committee" proposals such as the one Hall advances.

Party Reforms

The most promising reform ideas would subsidize those institutions that have incentives to solve collective action problems for individuals who might not otherwise be active in politics. Although historically there have been various kinds of institutions that have done this (see Skocpol 2003, for example), the most obvious modern candidate for such an institution is the political party. Parties have incentives to direct money to competitive races, to draw more people into politics, and to seek out and elevate promising candidates who might not be able to run competitive races on their own.

Since the late 1960s, however, parties have been increasingly limited in their ability to carry out these functions. Some of these limits arose from changing technologies (such as the rise of television and later the internet) that prompted campaigns to be more 'candidate-centered.' Some of the restrictions have been legal, however: parties have been limited in the amounts of money they can collect from contributors, in the extent to which they coordinate with candidates, and in how much they can independently spend in support of a candidate.

To be sure, parties have reinvented themselves as "service organizations" that remain important to many candidates (Aldrich 1995). But by operating like centralized consultancies, parties mostly facilitate the success of candidates that have already proved able to solve the collective action problems involved in campaign funding. Parties are highly restricted in the extent to which they can solve collective action problems for their candidates by financing their campaigns directly. These restrictions should be lifted.

***

Political parties are not very popular with the American public, however, and proposed relaxation of spending and contribution limits for them will be politically difficult to enact. Legitimate concerns about corruption would require stringent disclosure and monitoring. But at the very least, it is a discussion worth having because it would refocus attention on the neglected ways in which the collective action problems inherent in fundraising distort the political process. These distortions are very unlike the distortions that most reformers presume exist, but in my view they are more important. There is too little – not too much – money in politics, and its distribution accentuates the power of the wealthy, the well organized, and the extreme.

Bibliography

Ackerman, Bruce and Ian Ayres. *Voting with Dollars: A New Paradigm for Campaign Finance*. New Haven: Yale University Press, 2004.

Adamany, David W. and George E. Agree. *Political Money: A Strategy for Campaign Financing in America*. Baltimore: Johns Hopkins University Press, 1975.

Aldrich, John H. "Rational Choice and Turnout." *American Journal of Political Science* 37: 246-278, 1993.

Aldrich, John H. *Why Parties?: The Origin and Transformation of Political Parties in America*. Chicago: University of Chicago Press, 1995.

Alexander, Herbert. *Financing the 1964 Election*. Princeton, NJ: Citizens Research Foundation, 1966.

Alexander, Herbert E. *Financing Politics: Money, Elections, and Political Reform*. Washington, DC: Congressional Quarterly Press, 1976.

American Political Science Association, "Toward a More Responsible Two-Party System," *American Political Science Review* Vol 44 Supplement (September 1950).

Andreoni, James. 1989. "Giving with Impure Altruism: Applications to Charity and Ricardian Equivalence," *Journal of Political Economy* 97: 1447-1458.

Andreoni, James. 1990. "Impure Altruism and Donations to Public Goods: A Theory of Warm-Glow Giving," *The Economic Journal* 100: 467-477.

Ansolabehere, Stephen, John M. de Figuerido and James M. Snyder, Jr. "Why is There So Little Money in U.S. Politics?," *Journal of Economic Perspectives* 17:1 (March 2003), pp. 105-130.

Appel, Joseph H. *The Business Biography of John Wanamaker, Founder and Builder*. New York: Macmillan, 1930.

Armstrong, Richard. *The Next Hurrah: The Communication Revolution in American Politics*. New York: Beech Tree Books, William Morrow & Company, 1988.

Austen-Smith, David. "Campaign Contributions and Access," *American Political Science Review* 89:3 (Sep. 1995), pp. 566-581.

Baker, Paula. "Campaigns and Potato Chips; or Some Causes and Consequences of Political Spending." *Journal of Policy History* 14:1 (2002), pp. 4-29.

Banfield, Edward C. and James Q. Wilson. *City Politics*. New York: Random House, 1963.

Bartels, Larry M. *Unequal Democracy: The Political Economy of the New Gilded Age*. Princeton: Princeton University Press, 2008.

Becker, Gary S. "Altruism, Egoism, and Genetic Fitness: Economics and Sociobiology," *Journal of Economic Literature* 14:3 (September 1976) pp. 817-826.

Blau, Peter. 1964. *Exchange and Power in Social Life*. New York: Wiley.

Brader, Ted. 2006. *Campaigning for Hearts and Minds: How Emotional Appeals in Political Ads Work*. Chicago, IL: University of Chicago Press.

Brown, Clifford W., Jr., Lynda Powell, and Clyde Wilcox. *Serious Money: Fundraising and Contributing in Presidential Nomination Campaigns*. New York: Cambridge University Press, 1995.

Bryan, Frank M. *Real Democracy: The New England Town Meeting and How it Works*. Chicago: University of Chicago Press, 2004.

Casey, Ralph D. "Campaign Propaganda," *Annals of the American Academy of Political and Social Science* Vol. 179 (May 1935), p. 104.

Cebula, Richard J., Gary C. Durden, and Patricia E. Gaynor. 2008. "The Impact of the Repeat-Voting-Habit Persistence Phenomenon on the Probability of Voting in Presidential Elections." *Southern Economic Journal* 75: 429-440.

Clark, Peter B. and James Q. Wilson. 1961. "Incentive Systems: A Theory of Organizations." *Administrative Science Quarterly* 6: 129-166.

Clawson, Dan, Alan Neustadtl, and Mark Weller. *Dollars and Votes: How Business Campaign Contributions Subvert Democracy*. Philadelphia: Temple University Press, 1998.

Congressional Quarterly, *Dollar Politics: The Issue of Campaign Spending*. Washington DC: Congressional Quarterly, Inc., 1971.

Corrado, Anthony, Thomas E. Mann, Daniel R. Ortiz, Trevor Potter, and Frank J. Sorauf. *Campaign Finance Reform: A Sourcebook*. Washington, DC: Brookings, 1997.

Croly, Herbert. *Marcus Alonzo Hanna: His Life and Work*. New York: MacMillan, 1912.

Dillon, Andrew and Michael G. Morris. "User Acceptance of New Information Technology:Theories and Models," Annual Review of Information Science and Technology 31 (1996), pp. 3-32.

Dwyre, Diana and Victoria A. Farrar-Myers. *Legislative Labyrinth: Congress and Campaign Finance Reform*. Washington, DC: CQ Press, 2001.

Ellis, Joseph J. *His Excellency: George Washington*. New York: Random House, 2004.

Erie, Steven P. *Rainbow's End: Irish-Americans and the Dilemmas of Urban Machine Politics, 1840-1985*. Berkeley: University of California Press, 1990.

Fenno, Richard F. *Home Style: House Members in Their Districts*. Boston: Little, Brown, 1978.

Ferguson, Thomas. *Golden Rule: The Investment Theory of Party Competition and the Logic of Money-Driven Political Systems*. Chicago: University of Chicago Press, 1995.

Fowler, James H. and Nicholas A. Christakis, "Dynamic Spread of Happiness in a Large Social Network: Longitudinal Analysis Over 20 Years in the Framingham Heart Study," *British Medical Journal* 337 (768): a2338 (December 2008).

Fiorina, Morris P. with Samuel J. Abrams and Jeremy Pope. *Culture War?: The Myth of a Polarized America*, Third Edition. New York: Longman, 2011.

Francia, Peter L. John C. Green, Paul S. Herrnson, Lynda W. Powell, and Clyde Wilcox. 2003. *The Financiers of Congressional Elections: Investors, Ideologues, and Intimates.* New York: Columbia University Press.

Frumkin, Peter. *Strategic Giving: The Art and Science of Philanthropy.* Chicago, IL: University of Chicago Press, 2006.

Gerber, Alan S. "Does Campaign Spending Work?: Field Experiments Provide Evidence and Suggest New Theory," *American Behavioral Scientist* 47:5 (Jan. 2004), pp. 541-574.

Gerber, Alan S., Donald P. Green, and Christopher W. Larimer, "Social Pressure and Voter Turnout: Evidence from a Large-Scale Field Experiment," *American Political Science Review* 102:1 (February 2008), pp. 33-48.

Graff, Henry F. *Grover Cleveland: The American Presidents Series.* New York: Times Books, 2008.

Granovetter, Mark S. "The Strength of Weak Ties," *American Journal of Sociology* 78:6 (May 1973), pp. 1360-1380.

Hall, Richard L. "Equalizing Expenditures in Congressional Campaigns: A Proposal," *Election Law Journal* 6:2 (2007), pp. 145-162.

Hall, Richard L. and Frank Wayman, "Buying Time: Moneyed Interests and the Mobilization of Bias in Congressional Committees." *American Political Science Review*, 84:3, (Sep. 1990), p. 797-820.

Heard, Alexander. *The Costs of Democracy.* Chapel Hill: The University of North Carolina Press, 1960.

Heclo, Hugh. "Campaigning and Governing: A Conspectus," in Norman J. Ornstein & Thomas E. Mann, Eds., *The Permanent Campaign and its Future.* Washington, DC: The American Enterprise Institute and The Brookings Institution, 2000.

Hibben, Paxton. *The Peerless Leader: William Jennings Bryan.* New York: Farrar & Rinehart, Inc., 1929.

Hildreth, Anne. 1994. "The Importance of Purposes in 'Purposive' Groups: Incentives and Participation in the Sanctuary Movement." *American Journal of Political Science* 38: 447-463.

Hirschman, Albert O. 1982. *Shifting Involvements: Private Interest and Public Action.* Princeton, NJ: Princeton University Press.

Horner, William T. *Ohio's Kingmaker: Mark Hanna, Man and Myth.* Athens, OH: Ohio University Press, 2010.

Jacobson, Gary C. "The Effects of Campaign Spending in Congressional Elections," *American Political Science Review* 72:2 (Jun. 1978), pp. 469-491.

Jacobson, Gary C. "The Effects of Campaign Spending in House Elections: New Evidence for Old Arguments," *American Journal of Political Science* 34:2 (May, 1990), pp. 334-362.

Johnson, Bertram.. "Individual Contributors: A Fundraising Advantage for the Ideologically Extreme?" *American Politics Research* 38:5 (Sep. 2010), pp. 890-908.

Kehl, James A. *Boss Rule in the Gilded Age: Matthew Quay of Pennsylvania.* Pittsburgh: University of Pittsburgh Press, 1981.

Kelley, Stanley, Jr. *Professional Public Relations and Political Power.* Baltimore: The Johns Hopkins Press, 1956.

King, Gary, Robert O. Keohane, & Sidney Verba. *Designing Social Inquiry: Scientific Inference in Qualitative Research.* Princeton: Princeton University Press, 1994.

Knoke, David and James R. Wood. *Organized for Action: Commitment in Voluntary Associations.* New Brunswick, NJ: Rutgers University Press, 1981.

LaRaja, Raymond J. and David L. Wiltse, "Don't Blame Donors for Ideological Polarization of Political Parties: Ideological Change and Stability Among Political Contributors, 1972-2008," *American Politics Research* 40:3 (2012) pp. 501-530.

Lesher, Stephen. *George Wallace: American Populist.* Cambridge, MA: Perseus Publishing, 1994.

Levendusky, Matthew. *The Partisan Sort: How Liberals Became Democrats and Conservatives Became Republicans.* Chicago: University of Chicago Press, 2009.

Lindahl, Wesley E. *Principles of Fundraising: Theory and Practice.* Sudbury, MA: Jones & Bartlett, 2010.

Mansbridge, Jane. *Beyond Adversary Democracy.* New York: Basic Books, 1980.

Marcus, George E. 2002. *The Sentimental Citizen: Emotion in Democratic Politics.* University Park, PA: The Pennsylvania State University Press.

McCarty, Nolan M., Keith T. Poole, and Howard Rosenthal. *Polarized America: The Dance of Ideology and Unequal Riches.* Cambridge, MA: MIT Press, 2006.

McChesney, Fred. *Money for Nothing: Politicians, Rent Extraction, and Political Extortion.* Cambridge, MA: Harvard University Press, 1997.

McGinniss, Joe. *The Selling of the President, 1968.* New York: Penguin Books, 1970.

Mercer, David. *Marketing*, Second Edition. Malden, MA: Blackwell, 1996.

Mitchell, William C. and Michael Munger, "Economic Models of Interest Groups: An Introductory Survey," *American Journal of Political Science*, 35:2 (1991), pp 512-546.

Moe, Terry M. *The Organization of Interests: Incentives and the Internal Dynamics of Political Interest Groups.* Chicago: University of Chicago Press, 1980.

Morgan, H. Wayne. *From Hayes to McKinley: National Party Politics 1877-1896.* Syracuse, NY: Syracuse University Press, 1969.

Newman, Bruce I. *The Mass Marketing of Politics: Democracy in An Age of Manufactured Images.* Thousand Oaks, CA: Sage Publications, 1999.

North, Douglass C.. "Structure and Performance: The Task of Economic History," *Journal of Economic Literature*, 16:3 (September 1978), pp. 963-978.

North, Douglass C. *Institutions, Institutional Change, and Economic Performance.* New York: Cambridge University Press, 1990.

Obama for America. *Change We can Believe In.* New York: Three Rivers Press, 2008.

Olson, Mancur. *The Logic of Collective Action: Public Goods and The Theory of Groups.* Cambridge, MA: Harvard University Press, 1965.

Opp, Karl-Dieter. 1986. "Soft Incentives and Collective Action: Participation in the Anti-Nuclear Movement." *British Journal of Political Science* 16: 87-112.

Opp, Karl-Dieter. 1989. *The Rationality of Political Protest: A Comparative Analysis of Rational Choice Theory*. Boulder, CO: Westview Press.

Overacker, Louise. *Money in Elections*. New York: Macmillan, 1932.

Owens, John R. "Money in Politics in California: Democratic Senatorial Primary, 1964," Study Eleven in Herbert Alexander, Ed. *Studies in Money in Politics, Volume II*. Princeton, NJ: Citizens Research Foundation, 1970.

Parker, David C. W. *The Power of Money in Congressional Campaigns: 1880-2006*. Norman, OK: University of Oklahoma Press, 2008.

Plouffe, David. *The Audacity to Win: How Obama Won and How We Can Beat the Party of Limbaugh, Beck, and Palin*. New York: Penguin Books, 2010.

Pollock, James Kerr. *Party Campaign Funds*. New York: Alfred A. Knopf, 1926.

Poole, Keith T. and Howard Rosenthal. *Congress: A Political-Economic History of Roll Call Voting*. New York: Oxford University Press, 1997.

Price, David E. *The Congressional Experience*. Boulder, CO: Westview Press, 2000.

Putnam, Robert D. *Bowling Alone: The Collapse and Revival of American Community*. New York: Simon & Schuster, 2000.

Riker William H. & Peter Ordeshook. 1968. "A Theory of the Calculus of Voting." *American Political Science Review* 79: 62-78.

Riordan, William L. *Plunkitt of Tammany Hall: A Series of Very Plain Talks on Practical Politics*. New York: Signet Classics, 1995 [1905].

Rosenstone, Steven J. and John Mark Hansen. *Mobilization, Participation, and Democracy in America*. New York: Macmillan, 1993.

Salisbury, Robert H. 1969. "An Exchange Theory of Interest Groups." *Midwest Journal of Political Science* 13: 1-32.

Schattschneider, E. E. *The Semisovereign People: A Realist's View of Democracy in America*. New York: Holt, Rinehart and Winston, 1960.

Schier, Steven E. *By Invitation Only: The Rise of Exclusive Politics in the United States*. Pittsburgh: University of Pittsburgh Press, 2000.

Schuessler, Alexander A. *A Logic of Expressive Choice*. Princeton: Princeton University Press, 2000.

Sirota, David. *Hostile Takeover: How Big Money and Corruption Conquered Our Government – and How We Take it Back*. New York: Crown Publishers, 2006.

Skocpol, Theda. *Diminished Democracy: From Membership to Management in American Civic Life*. Norman, OK: University of Oklahoma Press, 2003.

Smith, Bradley A. *Unfree Speech: The Folly of Campaign Finance Reform*. Princeton, NJ: Princeton University Press, 2001.

Smith, Hedrick. *The Power Game: How Washington Works*. New York: Random House 1996 [1988].

Smith, Mark A. *American Business and Political Power: Public Opinion, Elections, and Democracy*. Chicago: University of Chicago Press, 2000.

Sorauf, Frank J. *Inside Campaign Finance: Myths and Realities*. New Haven: Yale University Press, 1992.

Steen, Jennifer A. *Self-Financed Candidates in Congressional Elections*. Ann Arbor: University of Michigan Press, 2006.

Stern, Philip M. *The Best Congress Money Can Buy*. New York: Pantheon, 1988.

Stratmann, Thomas. "What Do Campaign Contributions Buy? Deciphering Causal Effects of Money and Votes," *Southern Economic Journal* , Vol. 57, No. 3 (Jan., 1991), pp. 606-620.

Subcommittee of the Committee on Privileges and Elections, United States Senate ("Kenyon Committee"), *Presidential Campaign Expenses*. Washington: U.S. Government Printing Office, 1921.

Summers, Mark W. "'To Make the Wheels Revolve We Must Have Grease': Barrel Politics in the Gilded Age," *Journal of Policy History* 14:1 (2002), pp. 49-72.

Truman, David B. *The Governmental Process: Political Interests and Public Opinion*. New York: Alfred A. Knopf, 1951.

Tuck, Richard. *Free Riding*. Cambridge, MA: Harvard University Press, 2008.

Verba, Sidney, Kay Lehman Schlozman, and Henry E. Brady. 1995. *Voice and Equality: Civic Voluntarism in American Politics*. Cambridge, MA: Harvard University Press.

Weinstein, Stanley. The Complete Guide to Fundraising Management, Third Edition. Hoboken, NJ: John Wiley & Sons, 2009.

Whiteley, Paul F. and Patrick Seyd. 2002. *High-Intensity Participation: The Dynamics of Party Activism in Britain*. Ann Arbor, MI: University of Michigan Press.

Williamson, Vanessa, Theda Skocpol, and John Coggin, "The Tea Party and the Remaking of Republican Conservatism," *Perspectives on Politics*, 9:1 (March 2011), pp. 25-43.

Wilson, James Q. 1995 [1974]. *Political Organizations*. Princeton, NJ: Princeton University Press.

Zernike, Kate. *Boiling Mad: Inside Tea Party America*. New York: Times Books, 2010.

Index

About the Book

Why do some 30 million people in the United States give money to political candidates and causes—even though most individual contributions are irrational from the perspective of a strict cost-benefit analysis? How do campaign fundraisers tap into potential donors' motivations? Exploring three decades of historical data and also drawing extensively on the insights of contemporary campaign directors and consultants, Bertram Johnson makes sense of why people give and considers what this means for the campaign finance system, and the quality of representation, in the United States.

Bertram N. Johnson is associate professor of political science at Middlebury College.